T4-AJW-615

Soundtracks

To the Memory of a Music Lover
E. C. H.
1918–1963

Soundtracks

A Study of Auditory Perception, Memory, and Valuation.

JEAN GABBERT HARRELL

PROMETHEUS BOOKS

Published 1986 by Prometheus Books
700 East Amherst Street, Buffalo New York 14215

Library of Congress Catalog Card Number: 85-63387
ISBN 0-87975-334-X

Printed in the United States of America

"*The [Taos] Indian singing, sings without words or vision. Face lifted and sightless, eyes half closed and vision-less, mouth open and speechless, the sounds arise in the chest. He will tell you it is a song of a man coming home from a bear hunt: or a song to make rain: or a song to make the corn grow: or even, quite modern, the song of the church bell on Sunday morning. . . .*

"*The dark faces stoop forward, in a strange race-dark-ness. . . . And the spirits of the men go out in the ether, vibrating in waves from the hot, dark, intentional blood, seeking the creative presence that hovers forever in the ether, seeking identification, following on down the mysterious rhythms of the creative pulse, on and on into the germinating quick of the maize that lies under the ground, there, with the throbbing, pulsing, clapping rhythm that comes from the dark, creative blood in man, to stimulate the tremulous, pulsating protoplasm in the seed-germ, till it throws forth its rhythms of creative energy into the rising blades of leaf and stem.*"

—D. H. Lawrence
Mornings in Mexico

Contents

Preface

Years of concern with the art of music and philosophical observations about it have convinced me that no progress beyond the present theoretical state of affairs can be made without singling out auditory perception for study in a new way. If there is a primacy to be found in auditory perception, the history of epistemology has ignored it; in method, psychological experimenters have not understood it; and in its most pervasive twentieth-century extensions (film music) philosophical aestheticians have passed it by. Yet there it has been all along, in what can be neither seen nor touched nor found in space, a source of profundity in human experience that defies all cultural relativism. Of philosophers who have attempted a theory of the musical work, only Roman Ingarden has proposed a theory by reference to sound alone.* But with twentieth century technology to lay it bare, it is time that auditory perception was given its due.

I am indebted to John Hospers, Kingsley B. Price, and David Raksin for helpful criticism of an earlier version of this essay, and also to strong encouragement of my venture from Milton C. Nahm, who, incidentally, drew my attention to the quotation from D. H. Lawrence.

---

* In *The Work of Music and the Problem of Its Identity*, forthcoming in English translation by Adam Czerniawski, edited by Jean G. Harrell (Berkeley: University of California Press, 1986).

9

Introduction

This essay is primarily concerned with one major criterion of artistic and aesthetic value—depth or profundity—and its rooting, in the case of music, indelibly and apparently solely in auditory perception. It deliberately avoids an attempt at a general theory of value, or at a general theory of artistic expression, and it implicitly argues against limits imposed upon aesthetic inquiry by theories that are established to apply to all "arts" and, without discrimination, to all sensory media. Justification for this is based in part on recognition that auditory perception is fully developed in humans well prior to either visual or significant tactual perception, and also in raising certain *genetic* questions about the origin and nature of aesthetic value. It involves recognition of an aesthetic value to be found in a certain kind of memory that has consistently been referred to as "depth," and that recent general theories of valuation and evaluation have not uncovered. As a matter of fact, the preponderance of examples in philosophy of art and aesthetic inquiry have been visual or visual/tactual.

In their search for conditions of aesthetic value that are either "intrinsic" or "instrumental," philosophers have concentrated either on what is "presented here and now" in immediate perception, or on future-oriented analyses. Within this consistent visual/tactual and present/future orientation, arguments against relativism of aesthetic judgment have been hard to come by, although some such arguments have been vigorously defended. In its genetic orientation toward the past and its concentration exclusively on auditory perception, this essay provides an argument against relativism of aesthetic judgment in auditory art in a way that has never before been suggested. In its defense of aesthetic value to be found in an essentially passive mind function, it will likely approach heresy to those who cling to the Romantic view of *any* artist working in *any* genre as an active "creator" of things whose aesthetic significance is future-oriented in the "new" and "original." Yet, through a kind of dissecting process, concentration put on one major aesthetic quality (depth) deriving from only one sense medium seems to yield far more explantory power than have either general theories of value or general theories of art.

In chapter four, both C. I. Lewis's general "analysis of knowledge and valuation" and Monroe Beardsley's general theory of artisitic evaluation are seen to fail in explicating or explaining the quality of depth, primarily in music but to some extent in any art genre. There is also an analysis of assumptions that any general theory of artistic expression must make to explain the primary logical difficulty encountered by Susanne Langer's theory of music as a "presentational symbol," and highlight problems that Albert Hofstadter has found in certain general accounts of "creativity." Beginning in chapter one with an elucidation of a primary spatial metaphor in music criticism that is partly semantic and partly psychological, this essay provides in chapter two a new interpretation of the comparative significance of two major works on music aesthetics: Edmund Gurney's *The Power of Sound* and Eduard Hanslick's *The Beautiful in Music*. It provides in chapter three, through detailed examples from synchronized soundtracks of motion pictures, an explanation of general failure of depth-attribution to music in an art that primarily appeals to visual, not to auditory perception. And it provides in chapter five not only an explanation to the historian of why the concept of musical genius appeared when and where it did, but an invitation radically to rethink the concepts of genius and creativity, at least in auditory art.

Contrast between the logical and the empirical as sources of knowledge has been central in the history of Western epistemology. In illustrating empirical sources of knowledge, however, it has not appeared important to draw significant distinctions between different sensory media. "Sense data" indiscriminately refers to the visual, tactual, auditory, gustatory, or to any other. But when we look at epistemological examples of sense data, they are most often drawn from visual, or secondarily from tactual sources. What we *hear* is seldom referred to. When hearing assumes primary position in philosophy, as in the writings of

Arthur Schopenhauer, we find ourselves transcending from the factual to speculative metaphysics.

It is easy enough to explain why hearing has not figured importantly in epistemological questions. Through a kind of auditory impacting, a blindfolded person may hear the presence of a door and avoid bumping into it. But generally, auditory perception is an even more crude indicator of the presence of nearby objects than is a blind man's stick. Position of objects at a distance is even more difficult to fix by hearing alone. It has, however, seemed comparatively unimportant in epistemology to consider which human sense medium, if any, develops first, or to ask whether any sense media develop or are operative prior to birth. It seems consistently to have been assumed that all sense perception begins at birth and that all particular sense data are contingent on particular circumstances of individuals. The distinction of *a posteriori* knowledge rests on an assumption of contingency of all sense perception. In accord with Kant's naming that which is "universal and necessary" as marks of the *a priori*,[1] it has been assumed that we can point to no particular sense perceptions that all humans necessarily or universally have. Such is the skeptical heritage of Western epistemology.

Recent determination that auditory perception is fully developed by the fifth prenatal month raises some questions in this regard. As attendant conditions of the development of any and every human being, sounds that a fetus hears continuously from its fifth to ninth developmental months may be considered to be universal (in Kant's sense of having "no exceptions") and necessary, at least where *necessary* is taken as a synonym for *universal*.[2] This should mean that these primary prenatal sounds are *a priori*. All humans, by virtue of the fact that they are human, can be known to have heard them.

On the other hand, if the *a posteriori* is that which is contingent on, or results from sense perception, then these sounds should be *a posteriori*. Although for our purposes it does not matter which term better identifies them, if they are called by either term at all, this peculiar situation serves as a starter for a reconsideration of auditory perception from more than a valuational, aesthetic view. It will lead to the identification of the so-called "problem of musical purism" as, at base, an epistemological as well as a valuational question. Those who, following interpretations of Ludwig Wittgenstein, believe that analysis of the "language of expression" has successfully resolved or dissolved the old problem will be seen simply to be begging the question. Moreover, the general assumption of aestheticians that there are only two sources of explanation of aesthetic value in music—*form* and *expression*—will be recognized to be seriously mistaken. Again, Hegelian or naturalistic theories such as John Dewey's, which locate aesthetic value in resolution of opposing forces, can be shown in the case of major aesthetic power of music to be simply false.

This inquiry into auditory perception will allow us to justify moving from descriptions and interpretations of musical works to their consistently positive or negative evaluations in a way that no previous theory has clearly or convincingly allowed us to do. It will explain why references to depth in music are not only always valuational, but always positive, and why contrary references to shallowness are always valuational, but always negative. It will explain consistent judging of film music as shallow in a way that is finally more than *ad hominem* impugning of the film score composer's capacities, or than finding fault with forms of film music that are dependent on things seen or other non-musical circumstances. It will explain how we can praise film music as (sometimes) powerfully expressive, while criticizing it simultaneously as musically shallow.

It will do more. It will explain better than previous theories have how music critics can make sense to their audiences through a metaphorical language that, to a logician, amounts either to muddleheadedness or to sheer nonsense. It will explain how philosophers can speak of things metaphysical from the point of view of a solipsist, or how they can simultaneously speak of the subjective *as* objective. It will explain how music is called a universal language, although no semiotic function can clearly or consistently be identified in it. It will suggest why music never evokes fear, and why the major emotional qualities attending it are seldom, if ever, pains to be avoided. It will explain why there is almost no descriptive valuational language other than metaphor to articulate the music critic's message.

More than one philosopher has appeared to be driving at the central point that underlies this explanation. In setting music aside as having something special to distinguish it from other arts,

Schopenhauer seemed to have been trying to isolate some such point. But in calling music a "copy" of the "pure will," he failed, through his apparent inability to free himself from the old mimetic notion of copy.[3] Susanne Langer again appeared to have been trying to isolate this point, but in her final definition of music as a "presentational symbol" also failed, in her apparent unquestioning deference to Ernst Cassirer's theory of symbolism.[4] Edmund Gurney, viewing himself as a scientist in search of necessary and sufficient conditions of the power of musical sound, was clearly trying to isolate a particular condition of this power that he yet could not find. And so, to complete what would otherwise be an incomplete explanation, he posited the existence of a "unique and isolated musical faculty" that alone "can judge of such matters."[5] Even his early reviewer, James Sully, suspected that this faculty was a *deus ex machina*.[6] Again, in speaking of the music of Beethoven in terms of "spiritual contexts," J. W. N. Sullivan appeared to have been trying to isolate a unique condition of musical power that his deference to a theory of expression yet could not identify.[7] In a similar vein, Beardsley most recently has spoken of a quality in music of "metaphysical continuation."

> The idea that music exemplifies—indeed, exploits and glories in— aspects of change that are among the most fundamental and pervasive characteristics of living seems to be true. . . . Because these patterns or modes of continuation are such general features of all experience, I . . . call them *metaphysical*. . . . What makes them metaphysical is just that they are shared by so much besides music. . . . [And] the metaphysical modes of continuation that are deeply apprehended in music must account for much of its capacity to move us."[8]

Even in this latest attempt to clarify the nature of musical expression, its explantory power is weak. Beardsley gives no reason why awareness of "pervasive characteristics of living" expressed in music explains music's "capacity to move us"—always, it seems, in a positive way. Surely there are many things wrong with metaphysical continuation as well as right with it. Once more, Beardsley seems to have been stopped by deference to the concept of expression, and therefore has not considered the possibility that "deeply apprehended modes of continuation" may not be *expressed* properties at all.

Perhaps the most stubborn question for all of aesthetics has been how to move from detailed descriptions and interpretations of works of art to the justification of their evaluation. Consistently, the assumption has been that there are no universal or intrinsic criteria of aesthetic value, that all such criteria are culturally contingent. Hence, to find justification for particular evaluations of particular works, it has appeared necessary to draw a relation of dependence of qualities found in the work upon something else that has intrinsic value external to it. In this, there have appeared to be two ways to understand them: either to relate these qualities to certain formal features taken themselves to be principles having intrinsic, invariable value, or to relate these qualities to objects or events in the space-time world, thus explaining their value as expression or representations of something else.

This something else, then, will be taken to possess intrinsic, invariant value, and the artwork's value will be taken to be derivative and dependent upon it. Both ways presuppose a source of value independent of the work, either in some kind of universal formal rule or in some pervasive feature of the real world. Neither of these routes succeeds, for the reason that neither demonstrates such intrinsic value in any formal rule, or in any independent features of the space-time world expressed or represented in the work. Even John Dewey's theory that locates aesthetic value in the *process* itself of connecting particular artworks with universal or pervasive features of human life, and in the "consummatory" aspects of any human experience, does not succeed. The stubborn question of how to move from descriptions and interpretations of "what we have here" to whether the thing is "any good" remains. But the clear and age-old power of music to move, to transport, to reach wellsprings of one's very being, supports a continued conviction that there *must* be something there, although we may be as convinced as was Eduard Hanslick that "this primitive and mysterious power . . . will forever be hidden from us."[9] Surely it is doubtful that logical analyses of critics or philosophers can determine what it is.

Immanuel Kant's solution to the general question was ingenious, but did not really resolve it. We might put Kant's answer in terms of semantic analysis of sentences or statements having different forms and functions. The characteristic aesthetic judgment takes the *form* of an Aristotelian proposition "S is P," where *beautiful* appears in predicate place, as in "The rose is beautiful." But the proposition does not *function* declaratively as an assertion of fact. It functions imperatively to say: "I demand that all men shall find it so."[10] By such analysis of language form and function, Kant could affirm that there is no universal concept—in the sense of universality in the *Critique of Pure Reason*—to be found determining aesthetic judgments; but he could also explain why it appears that there must be such a concept. Yet, however ingenious this solution was, it clearly involved changing the meaning of *universality* and *necessity*, a fact that Kant himself acknowledged. It may indeed be the case that when I say "Beethoven's music is deep," I am demanding that all men shall find it so. But simply distinguishing the form from the function of my sentence is not adequate explanation of my demand. When Schopenhauer said— as have many others—that music is a universal language, we look for an explication of this claim without changing the meaning of universal. We want an explication in which universal means what it meant to Kant in the *Critique of Pure Reason*, not in the *Critique of Judgment*. Music may not literally be a language, but rather, very like a language. Yet, the claim to universality of understanding is made in the function as well as in the form of a declarative, true statement, whether music is literally a language or not. The claim of Schopenhauer was one of what all men in fact *do* understand, and of what all men also in fact sympathize with. No linguistic or logical analysis promises to account for this.

Topics of aesthetic analysis, which have been extensively pursued and are most popular, appear to be just those that are amenable to logical or linguistic analysis rather than to psychological observations about different sensory media—topics on the nature of expression, representation, style, form, structure, meaning, or semantics. Yet finally, the world that aesthetics seeks to analyze is ineradicably a world of delight in sight and sound and touch. It would have been thought, however, that general aesthetic distinctions relating to sight, for example, should also relate to sound, or to touch; that general principles of expression or form should apply equally well to any art addressing any sense medium. Understanding one of the most fundamental evaluations of auditory art, however, demonstrates the irrelevance of general analyses of expression or of representation, the irrelvance of style, the irrelevance of technical formal distinctions, and the irrelevance of logical techniques for clarifying metaphorical language of music critics—in short the irrelevance of nearly every subject recently dear to the hearts of philosophical aestheticians. Standing as an exception is Ingarden's piece on the musical work in volume two of *Studia z estetyki* (*Studies of Aesthetics*). Although his inquiry was primarily into the ontological status and identity of a musical work rather than into grounds of its positive or negative evaluation (as ours), Ingarden's concentration solely on sound yielded observations about specifically auditory art that come close to recognizing primary points raised in this essay.

NOTES

1. *Critique of Pure Reason*, B4.

2. Richard Robinson finds four meanings of *necessity* to be indiscriminately mixed by Kant in the first *Critique*, one of which identifies *necessity* as *universality*. "Necessary Propositions," *Mind* 67, no. 267 (July 1958):209–304. Reprinted in Penelhum and Macintosh, *The First Critique* (Belmont, Calif.: Wadsworth, 1969).

3. See Arthur Schopenhauer, *The World as Will and Idea*, translated by R. B. Haldane and J. B. Kemp, (New York: Charles Scribner's Sons, 1950).

4. See *Philosophy in a New Key* (Cambridge, Mass.: Harvard University Press, 1942), ch. 8.

5. See restatement in "The Psychology of Music," *Mind* 7 (1882): 89–100.

6. Review of *The Power of Sound* in *Mind* 6 (1881):287.

7. See *Beethoven: His Spiritual Development* (New York: Vintage, 1927).

8. "Understanding Music," in *On Criticizing Music: Five Philosophical Perspectives*, edited by Kingsley Price, (Baltimore, Md.; London: Johns Hopkins University Press, 1981), 70, 71.

9. *The Beautiful in Music*, translated by Gustav Cohen, (New York: Liberal Arts, Bobbs-Merrill, 1957), 52.

10. *Critique of Judgment, Analytic of the Beautiful*, especially ¶ 6–9.

One

Depth Metaphor in Music Criticism

Twentieth century aestheticians still uniformly reflect Kant's distinction between philosophical and psychological inquiry. As philosophers, they typically regard their inquiry as logical rather than psychological, as what might be considered a twentieth century extension, via Wittgenstein, of Kant's *Critique of Judgment*. This study centers on logical analysis of the language of art critics, and has often been termed *metacriticism*. But it will be remembered that, early in the *Critique of Pure Reason* (*CPR*), Kant thought that such *aesthetic* inquiry was not possible. In A21, he termed Baumgarten's attempt "abortive" and "fruitless." What Baumgarten called "aesthetics" and others called "critique of taste" was bound to yield empirical psychology, not transcendental principles. Kant, however, modified this footnote in the second edition of *CPR* (B36), indicating that aesthetics *might* be partially "transcendental" and partially "psychological." This present inquiry may easily be taken as an example of Kant's earlier modified view of aesthetics prior to writing the *Critique of Judgment*. The particular inquiry here, which initally looks like a phase of logical analysis of language of music critics, unavoidably includes speculative psychology to such an extent that the result is a hybrid. Why is this result unavoidable and what does this philosophical-psychological tack have to recommend it?

When we look at the art of music, we recognize two primary languages. The first is the language of music theoreticians, rooted in the visually accessible notational system that Nelson Goodman has had in mind,[1] and in the metanotational systems, again visually accessible, of theoreticians such as Jean Philippe Rameau, with his Roman numerals and Arabic numbers,[2] or as Heinrich Schenker, with his long horizontal lines indicating an *Urlinie*.[3] Some of this language may also, in a secondary way, be tactually determined, as in the principles of voice-leading in four-part harmony of C. P. E. Bach and his father, where keyboard fingering possibilites were of paramount importance.[4] It is this notational and metanotational language that is most easily recognized as descriptive, or as interpretative in a way clearly and logically analyzable even by one who is tone-deaf.

There is a second language of music criticism that is not visually or tactually accessible, which is rooted in audition, and which consists almost entirely of spatial metaphor. This is the language that is best candidate for the appellation "aesthetic," and is the language whose clarification depends on a technique of elucidation reaching beyond that of strict logical analysis. Philosophers have devised various theories of what any metaphor is, but the techniques characteristic of metacriticism in aesthetics viewed as philosophy (after Kant's later view) themselves offer little or no promise in fulfilling the task of metaphorical elucidation. Success can no longer be found if we are tone-deaf. We must, it seems, move into empirical observations specifically about auditory perception, to the exclusion of what can be seen or touched and checked in the spatial world. We must move into the mercurial and mysterious world of audition.

Difficulty of analyzing metaphor in music criticism may be traced in large measure to the fact that musical works known by audition have no spatial location. It makes no sense to ask *"Where is Ravel's Bolero?,"* although it does make sense to ask *"When did Ravel's Bolero come into being?"* A musical work *may* be known visually by looking at its score (which, of course, is spatially located), or tactually, as when we may say of a composer who is a keyboardist that the structure of his composition is determined partly by keyboard performance possibilities and that he "brought his composition under his fingers." But primary metaphor in music criticism appears to draw connections between what is heard and aspatial, and what is known mainly through visual-tactual perception and is spatial. This seems to be the commonest kind of metaphor in music criticism and it is also the most difficult to explicate. Prominent in this kind is what I shall call "depth metaphor." Gurney used depth metaphor in observing that, throughout the lives of many people, music retains "the monopoly of stirring [them] to the depths."[5] Schopenhauer again used depth metaphor when he observed in *The World as Will and Idea* that "Music restores to us all the emotions of our inmost nature, but entirely without reality and far removed from their pain." The primary depth metaphor in this quotation is in the word *inmost*. Gurney used *stirring* as well as depths. Another common depth metaphor is *wellsprings*.

Certain preliminary things should be noticed about depth metaphor in music criticism. First, its function is always more than descriptive; it is always valuational as well, and in a positive way. In other words, there is always something good, indeed as good as anything can be, in "deep music." This differs from references to musical expression or symbol, which are not always valuational in a positive way, as when we refer to hackneyed expression or symbolization in film music. Second, depth metaphor in music criticism does not connote something expressed, represented, or symbolized, however these terms are understood. Third, depth metaphor in music criticism always includes reference to an emotional state, but to an emotional state that may be called undifferentiated—that is, one which cannot be distinguished as any particular emotion which is different from other emotions. To say "Beethoven's music is deep" always includes the "stirring of deep emotion." This may not be all that is connoted in saying that Beethoven's music is deep, but it appears to be an invariant part of the metaphor. Fourth, the connection drawn by depth metaphor between music and spatial circumstances is not accidental or contingent, as associations drawn individually, or conventions determined socially, seem to be. Associations or conventions might have been other than they are, but connotation of depth metaphor in music criticism seems to be of an emotional condition of anything that is human, regardless of particular circumstances that may differ from one human or group of humans to another. Thus, depth in music is not taken to be dependent on style, or on relative complexity or simplicity of structure; and there can be no such thing as deep music that is hackneyed or in bad taste.

Now, how do we elucidate such metaphor? Let us begin with a casual observation. When a minister says to his parish, "Let us pray silently," he does not add, "and let us plug our ears." He may be able to be sure that his congregation will bow their heads and close their eyes, and that their hands will at the moment not be reaching out to explore the spatial world. This should make it easier to contact universals without the distracting sight of a lady's hat with red cherries in the front pew or the need manually to get rid of that offending object. But surely, in communing with things ontological, accompanying organ music is perfectly appropriate, not a deterrent at all. The congregation may automatically tune out distant sounds of auto horns or of overhead planes; but music during otherwise silent prayer is not *supposed* to be tuned out. Why? We may hear echoes of Hume's voice in answer: "'Tis custom. 'Tis convention. 'Tis formed by constant contiguity."

We may also note that prayer and religion are usually concerned not only with things universal, but also with things universally human—that is, with birth and death, and with what goes on in life after the social accidents, especially the pains, have been wiped away. Can there be something in audition of music that functions like a foundation (hence the depth metaphor) upon which accidents are both built and erased, something elemental, something primordially human? If there is, then the use of music during otherwise silent prayer is not itself an accident, be it of individual association or of social custom. It may well be a means of recollection of what is so far back in time as to have been forgotten, but also recollection of a conscious and feeling state originally known through hearing alone, prior to having seen or touched anything.* Depth metaphor in music criticism appears to draw a relation between what is temporally remote and known solely by audition with what has spatial location but is not visually or tactually accessible. Depth terminology in its literal reference to spatial circumstance is often of that which cannot, momentarily at least, be seen or touched. What is deep is often not visible, although perhaps if I dig down far enough it will become so. What I stir up of a mixture from the bottom of a pot may easily not have been visible. Wellsprings are not visible except to one who goes down there. The unborn infant who is "inner" is visible to outsiders only by the bulge that he creates. And the keyboard composer may literally bring his composition under his fingers,

---

* Minimal tactual perception may be assumed prenatally when a fetus can touch its body with its hand or on occasion suck its thumb. We may find in prayer analogous sensations in such as the telling of beads.

but I may say that his composition "touches something that I can't put my finger on."

There is, it seems, a strong relation between depth metaphor in music criticism and equally common metaphorical references to the "depths of memory." Experiences, at least of anything that we consciously remember, have been in the spatial as well as in the temporal and aspatial dimension. Has there ever been a time when we had auditory perception and not yet visual/tactual perception? The answer to this question, of course, is yes.

The theory that I propose, which I shall call a theory of partial recall, may at the outset appear to be implausible, even outrageous. But in the end it will not only serve to explicate depth metaphor in music criticism. It will also provide a basis for explaining far more than this particular metaphor. It will suggest answers to outstanding questions in music aesthetics that theories of expression or symbolization or representation do not and, I think, cannot answer. They cannot, it seems, primarily because they all require that a distinction be drawn between qualitative and numerical identity.

To refer to memory in explication of depth metaphor marks a move out of logical or linguistic analysis of metaphor into speculative psychology. Now, I admit that I do not know what memory is. Worse, explanations by reference to unconscious memory are surely open to the criticism that they are not, in principle, refutable. The theory must live with these problems, but in the hope of finding answers to major outstanding aesthetic questions, it is still worth pursuing.

We are well acquainted with Marcel Proust's observations about memory. Through the taste of cake dipped in tea, Proust's recall of Sunday mornings in Combray depended primarily on gustatory and visual perceptions. Thus:

> Many years had elapsed during which nothing of Combray . . . had any existence for me, when one day in winter as I came home, my mother, seeing that I was cold, offered me some tea, a thing I did not ordinarily take. . . . I raised to my lips a spoonful of the tea in which I had soaked a morsel of the cake. No sooner had the warm liquid, and the crumbs with it, touched my palate than a shudder ran through my whole body. . . . An exquisite pleasure had invaded my senses. . . . Whence could it have come to me, this all-powerful joy? . . . And suddenly the memory re-

turns. The taste was that of the little crumb of "madeleine" which on Sunday mornings at Combray . . . my Aunt Léonie used to give me, dipping it first in her own cup of real or of limeflower tea. . . . Immediately the old grey house upon the street rose up like the scenery of a theatre . . . so in that moment all the flowers in our garden in M. Swann's park, and the water-lillies on the Vivonne and the good folk of the village and their little dwellings and the parish church and the whole of Combray and of its surroundings, taking their proper shapes and growing solid, sprang into being, town and gardens alike, from my cup of tea.[6]

Certain similarities and differences should be noted between auditory memory and Proust's connections of taste and vision. As depth metaphor in music criticism does not connote something resulting from association or convention, Proust's apparent total recall of that earlier time and place is not adequately explained by a theory of association or constant contiguity. Proust did not simply associate the taste of the madeleine cake with the particular look of Combray. Rather, the taste of the cake in tea was a *part of* the memory. The connection was, however, accidental in a way that connotation of depth metaphor in music criticism is not. Proust's not only became a conscious recollection, but the joy he found fused in it was differentiated—that is, distinguishable from other nameable emotions. And, of course, Proust's memory was of things in space as well as time.

In his chapter, "Sounds," in *Individuals*, P. F. Strawson raised an epistemological question about auditory perception. If our sole sense perception were auditory, would we distinguish the qualities of our perception from ourselves, or, indeed, from anything producing them? Could we, as Strawson put it, distinguish qualitative from numerical identity?[7] Now, Strawson would undoubtedly agree that he was not doing speculative psychology. Indeed, he doubted that any such state of purely auditory experience was possible.

We drew a picture of a purely auditory experience, and elaborated it to a point at which it seemed that the being whose experience it was—if any such being were possible at all—might recognize sound-universals and reidentify sound-particulars and in general form for himself an idea of his auditory world; but still, it seemed he would have no place for the idea of himself as the subject of this experience, would make no distinction between a special item in his world, namely himself, and the other items in it. Would it not seem utterly strange to suggest that he might distinguish himself as one item among others in his auditory world, that is, as a sound or sequence of sounds? For how could such a thing—a sound—be also what *had* all those experiences?[8]

In *The Foundations of Empirical Knowledge*, A. J. Ayer makes the same point in a somewhat different way.[9]

In positing a solipsistic state in one whose sole data were auditory, neither Strawson nor Ayer considered the close analogy to just this state in prenatal existence, one in which audition is fully developed by the fifth gestational month, but one in which we presume other sensory media are yet undeveloped. Recently, a recording was made of the primary sounds that an unborn fetus hears continuously from its fifth to ninth months of development—that is, for almost half of its gestational period.[10] When this recording is played back to newborn infants, the results are uniform to measured seconds: In thirty seconds crying stops, and in sixty seconds the infant is asleep. His face often wears what might be called a smile of beatitude.

One may distinguish three phases in this prenatal sound complex. The first and probably most obvious is a hammering sound, having a slight echo, that is apparently produced by the systolic phase of the heart beat. This makes the complex of sounds resemble those of a distant construction project. The second is of a rushing sound apparently produced by the coursing of blood through vessels. The third consists of two separate sounds, the first slightly louder, that are apparently produced by the diastolic phase of the heart beat. If the tones Eb and Db are played on a piano in the same rhythmic configuration, and the recording is then repeated, our ears will move these sounds into those pitches.

Now, one may easily find aspects of different kinds of music that *can* be interpreted as auditory analogues of this entire prenatal complex, or of parts of it. But evidence that hearing an analogy may produce and then become a part of total or partial recall of the prenatal state is only indirect. Before proceeding with two illustrations, it is important to note that auditory analogues in these illustrations are not taken to function as sufficient conditions of a total or partial recall, any more than the taste of cake dipped in tea guaranteed that Proust would always experience the particular recollection that he had on one occasion. Neither is a presumed recall through auditory analogue taken as a guarantee that a description of it will include one or another depth metaphor. The following illustrations are given to make it plausible that aspects of music, probably by auditory analogue, may trigger partial or total recall of a prior human state known in conjunction with auditory, but not with visual/tactual perception.

The first and probably most obvious illustration is found in the typical tone-rhythm configuration of a lullaby. This configuration may be interpreted as an auditory analogue of the diastolic phase of the prenatal sound complex. Among the most obvious examples are in *Rock-A-Bye-Baby* and Chopin's *Berceuse* (Opus 57). Now, it seems clear that this tone rhythm configuration of a lullaby is not deemed suitable to use by social custom or individual association. An infant cannot be aware of either. The practical effects of a lullaby may be the same as that of hearing the recording of the prenatal sounds, although they may be longer in coming. One may then argue with some plausibility that the auditory analogue in the typical lullaby of diastolic prenatal sounds produces a recall of a prenatal state for the infant, who is thus lulled to sleep. This result may be obtained, as in the next illustration, by a combination of at least one other factor with an auditory analogue, in this case with a rocking cradle.

As a second illustration, a startling likeness to the entire prenatal sound complex may be found in a type of Jamaican music called "reggae," which, together with marijuana, is used as a religious sacrament by members of a cult known as Rastafarianism. Indeed, many reggaes may be interpreted as little else. They contain the same hammering sound (often with slight echo), an insistent syncopated back beat that may take the place of the prenatal rushing sound, and the same downward whole-tone drop characterizing the diastolic phase of the heart beat. The typical picture of a Rastafarian, who is relaxed by marijuana and listening to reggae, is of one whose eyes are closed, or nearly closed, whose body is inert, and who wears the same smile of beatitude as that of the infant hearing once more the prenatal sounds. The Rastafarian is literally "spaced out." Now, we outsiders may hardly be expected to call reggae music deep. But it is likely that the Rastafarian, hearing it in combination with the effects of marijuana, would call it just that. Indeed, when lyrics have been added to reggae, we find judgments about what words are appropriate and inappropriate quite in accord with depth metaphor. Thus, one Joe Higgs, who has been named Senior Dean of Reggae, finds the following words decidedly inappropriate for reggae: "Baby, I love you—let me take you out in my Cadillac." Rather, he finds lyrics appropriate that draw no distinction between qualitative and numerical identity. Higgs, himself a Rastafarian, details his religious insight—to the probable outrage of a logician—thus: "Love is life, and life is God. If life is God, then everyone alive should be in the same awareness—a rainbow of consciousness."[11]

We come now to music which is uniformly described as deep by human beings who have long since forgotten what they have heard before birth, and who have neither cradles nor marijuana to boost *some* recall. It may be that certain aspects of this music, most likely auditory analogues, trigger a partial recall of very early auditory experience, had independently of visual/tactual perception, which is not consciously recognized for what it is. This may be presumed to be an experience having a positive emotional (undifferentiated) quality consistent with what might be called "the dynamics of being alive," but one not yet faced with Hegelian "challenges" in the space-time world. The fetus, after all, is not in want. It is not cold. It is not hungry. All conditions needed to promote its vigorous development are provided. It cannot see, cannot touch except in a very minimal way. But it can hear. Who is to say that this very early prenatal *gestalt* is not in certain auspicious circumstances at least dimly remembered yet only expressible through metaphorical language drawn from the spatial world that does not separate or even distinguish the feelings of the aesthetic judge from the qualities of things heard? What is found, then, would not be a result of symbolic, expressive, or representational functions. Like the taste of Proust's cake, musical sounds may become a part of a total or partial recall, either taking the place of, or underlining some or all of the prenatal sound complex.

We should think that in music uniformly and unanimously called deep—for example, in a great deal of the music of Beethoven—it would be farfetched to try to spell out any such analogues in detail; indeed, that any such attempt could do no service to the genius of this composer. Yet to our astonishment,

we may find, for example, in the *Coriolan* overture (Opus 62)—
and, of course heavily depending upon the particular interpretation—an analogy so close in rhythm, tone configuration, and pace
throughout the composition that at times, when they are super-
imposed, the prenatal sounds and the orchestral performance
seem to merge as though into one composition. In this particular
example, the analogy is closer, more obvious and consistent than
is that of any lullaby or of much Jamaican reggae. Yet it is the
depth that Beethoven's music reaches, perhaps more than any
other of its qualities, that puts this composer at the top in majority
opinion. Not only can we repeatedly find this analogy in a sub-
stantial amount of Beethoven's music. We may conversely point
to music bearing no analogy, either in rhythm, tone configuration,
or pace as also music that is *not* described or evaluated as "deep"—
for example, Gregorian Chant, in which there is no percussive
"beat-to-the-bar" rhythm, and the tonal direction is determined
by the text.

Still, if this explanation of depth metaphor in music criticism
is correct, explication of the metaphor in particular uses probably
should remain indeterminate. We will have to be content with
metaphor. Linguistically, we will still be understood if we remain
"unable to put our finger on it." After all, we may momentarily
"be in touch" with a state that was pre-linguistic as well as pre-
visual and tactual. Rather than attempting to be precise and literal,
we may do better by asking a rhetorical question: "Can't you just
hear it?" Or perhaps in desperation we may use vocabulary like
Joe Higgs's and talk about the music as being "universally human,"
or erase any difference between physical bodily feelings and the
universal, as Rastafarians do, who think that Haile Selassie was
God and that Jesus Christ is a live, physical human presence
whom you may meet sometime. We may thus enrage logicians by
talking about "being and consciousness," and suffer hearing them
say once more: "We don't know what you mean!" The core of our
problem would be a result precisely that Strawson and Ayer at
least suggested—an inability through logic, language, and public
communication to describe a solipsistic state. The built-in distinction between subject and predicate should prevent this.

So, then, what are the questions that this theory of partial
recall suggests answers to which other theories of music do not?

1. Why do music critics in their most enthusiastic judgments consistently fail to distinguish between feelings had and an object described?

2. Why is there almost no language other than spatial metaphor to articulate the music critic's aesthetic message?

3. Why is one of the most powerful emotional qualities of music regarded as something primordially human, rather than accidental?

4. Why does clarification of meaning of the terms *expression, symbolization,* or *representation* in music still fail to resolve or dissolve the so-called "problem of musical purism?"

5. Why does music never evoke fear? (Note here that the answer does not need now to be made by reference to "psychical distance," or to "make-believe.")

6. Why is one of the most powerful emotional qualities of music not differentiated as some particular emotion, such as might be a response to particular space-time circumstances?

7. Why does music sometimes bring tears in a way that visual perceptions to not? Neither Hogarth's "perfectly beautiful line" nor "that certain gorgeous shade of pink" brings tears. (Note that it is neither full harmony nor a complete melody which does this, but rather a certain "turn" in a melody.)

8. Why is it said that music is a ticket to freedom? What can be meant by freedom?

9. Why is music consistently used in religious services when, at least in prayer, vision is deliberately cut out? And why is sound not cut out in Moslem prayer when the entire body assumes a fetal-like position and nobody in that position can possibly *see* anything—except perhaps, if he peeks, the threads of a prayer rug.

10. Why does music seem so important in provoking and/or underlining nostalgia?

In the light of Strawson's and Ayer's inquiries into auditory perception, it is not surprising that almost every illustration of knowledge sources in epistemology has been visual or visual/

tactual, from the straight stick that looks bent in water, to the dimensions of the coin in Bertie Russell's pocket. It is small wonder that even the bulk of aesthetic inquiry addresses vision or that which involves vision. And it is small wonder that visually-spatially oriented analyses of artistic expression trade on, indeed, require a distinction to be made between feelings had by persons and numerically distinct objects described in terms of those feelings. Yet such analysis can only explain depth metaphor in music criticism as harboring a logical confusion. If such weak explanation is then given legislative power, the critic using depth metaphor may be told by the analyst to clean up his logical act. It should not, then, be surprising if the critic responds either that the analyst's understanding of the subject is shallow—a metaphor contrary to deep, and in literal reference accessible to vision—or that he does not understand the metaphor at all.

Elucidation of critical metaphor should be considered a perfectly viable phase of theory of art criticism. But when that art is music and accessible by audition, rather than by visual or tactual perception, then the most productive method yields just what Kant originally thought would characterize all aesthetics as Baumgarten viewed it: a theoretical hybrid that is partially logical and partially psychological. At least in explication of this particular and pervasive spatial metaphor of "depth," no other way seems to have been open. If this elucidation of a primary critical criterion of maximum positive value in music is correct, as we shall see in greater detail in chapter four, it deals a painful blow to relativism in aesthetics.

NOTES

1. See *Languages of Art* (New York: Bobbs-Merrill, 1968).

2. Jean Philippe Rameau, *Traité de l'Harmonie Réduite a ses Principes Naturels* (1722); *Démonstration du Principe de l'Harmonie (1750); Nouvelles Réflections sur la Démonstration du Principe de l'Harmonia* (1752). [*Treatise on Harmony Reduced to Its Natural Principles* (1722); *Principles of Harmony* (1750); and *New Reflections on the Principles of Harmony* (1752)].

3. See *Neue musikalische Theoreien und Phantasien* [*New Musical Theories and Fantasies*], 3 vols., Heinrich Schenker, artist facsimile reprint edited by Lothar Hoffmann-Erbrecht, (Leipzig: Breitkopf & Härtel, 1957).

4. See C. P. E. Bach, *Versuch über die wahre Art das clavier zu spielen.* English translation with Introduction by William J. Mitchell, *Essay on the True Art of Playing Keyboard Instruments* (New York: W. W. Norton & Co., Inc., 1949).

5. Edmund Gurney, *The Power of Sound* (London: Smith, Elder, & Co., 1880), 368.

6. Marcel Proust, *Swann's Way,* translated by C. K. Scott Moncrieff. (New York: Modern Library, 1928, 1956).

7. *Individuals* (New York: Doubleday-Anchor, 1963), 61.

8. Ibid., 82, 83.

9. See *The Foundations of Empirical Knowledge* (London: Macmillan & Co., Ltd.; New York: St. Martin's Press, 1963), 253–255.

10. Marketed by The Rushton Company, Atlanta, Georgia, under the name *Rock-A-Bye-Baby, Inc.,* 1975. Recording made by Dr. William C. Eller at Holy Cross Hospital, Fort Lauderdale, Florida.

11. Michael Snyder, "Joe Higgs—Senior Dean of Reggae," *Datebook, The San Francisco Examiner-Chronicle* (October 18, 1981):29.

Two

A Case for Edmund Gurney

Although the strong and immediately affective power of music has been recognized over the centuries, analysis or explanation of it has not appeared to connect with epistemology, with theory of knowledge. Affective responses to music have generally been regarded as irrational and as unguided by any invariant rule—at least by any rule that is discoverable—such as would govern the acquisition of knowledge of what is true or false about the space-time world. We may even pursue the science of acoustics, or the theory of Rameau, that would root music in mathematical principles, and still fail to find principles governing affective responses to music in an invariant or universal way. In the face of such clear recognition, we find persistent claims to universality of musical "understanding" among all humans as a fact that will thus forever remain unexplained. If we cannot explain these claims, however, it may appear that we can explain them away. Perhaps if we understand the logistics of language in the aesthetic field generally, we can finally dissolve these claims as linguistic in origin, and as only apparently claims to *facts* about anything at all.

Two nineteenth-century authors have most frequently been referred to as providing starting points for inquiries into music aesthetics: Eduard Hanslick and Edmund Gurney. Of the two, Hanslick was more clearly the logician and language analyst, while Gurney was the astute empirical observer. When language analysis has taken precedence over empirical psychology over the last decades in philosophical aesthetics, it should thus be expected that, where any nineteenth-century theory is mentioned at all, Hanslick's *On the Beautiful in Music* would be favored over Gurney's *The Power of Sound*. Many critics have attested to

Gurney's "brilliant observations," but his method, together with his often long and loose sentences and inexact vocabulary, have undoubtedly contributed to the virtual eclipse of *The Power of Sound* since its publication over a century ago. Sitting down to read the 559 pages of *The Power of Sound* is a little like sitting down to read *War and Peace*. Immediate comprehension is not to be forthcoming.

Monroe C. Beardsley aptly chose quotations from Hanslick's book indicating his semantic approach to the question of musical signification.

> Eduard Hanslick's penetrating and witty work I interpret as in part a thorough refutation of earlier and less sophisticated forms of the Signification Theory. "The forest is cool and shady, but it certainly does not represent [stellt nicht dar] the feeling of cool-ness and shadiness"; again, "Epithets . . . may be used so long as we remain fully conscious of their figurative sense—nay, we may even be unable to avoid them; but let us never say, 'This piece of music *expresses* [*shildert*] pride, etc.', and 'It is aesthetically quite correct to speak of a theme as having a sad or noble accent, but not as expressing [*nicht aber, es sei ein Ausdruck der*] the sad or noble feelings of the composer." Despite terminological lapses, e.g., some puzzling remarks on "symbolism," this position is con-sistently and vigorously maintained throughout the book.[1]

We might add to Beardsley's selections other logical references of Hanslick, i.e., that conditions discussed "would be a contradiction in terms" (p. 37), "would be arguing in a circle" (p. 39), would be "logically compelling" (p. 39), would be insufficient "proof" (p. 40), or would be "impossible" (p. 46). We may then compare excerpts from Gurney's book to note a clear difference in method between these two authors. Here is a typical reason given for Gurney's argument: "A musical child may feel the overmastering magic of Beethoven before the shadows or conflicts of life have any existence for him."[2] Now we do not appeal to principles of logic or of linguistic meaning, and there is no logical issue here. We want, rather, to know whether what Gurney says is in fact true. Most probably our means to verify his statement are to introspect and to remember.

Did *we*, as musical children, feel the overmastering magic of Beethoven before the shadows or conflicts of life had any existence for us? Our answer will probably be a resounding "yes!" Again, in his argument against emotional "expression" as either a necessary or a sufficient condition of musical "impressiveness," Gurney noted a difference in certain strong emotions attending musical experiences: "So far as it can be described, it seems like a fusion of strong emotions transfigured into a wholly new experience, whereof if we seek to bring out the separate threads we are hopelessly baulked; for triumph and tenderness, desire and satisfaction, yielding and insistence, may seem to be there all at once, yet without any dubiousness or confusion in the result; or rather elements seem there which we struggle dimly to adumbrate by such words, thus making the experience seem vague only by our own attempt to analyze it. . . ."[3] Here we have an implicit recognition that there are two ways to identify vagueness—linguistic and experiential. The "strong emotion" that Gurney tried to identify by logically contrary words must be recognized by the one who has had it, and knows it in an *experientially* exact way. This differs from the precision or vagueness of the words that are available to describe it.

Undoubtedly the methods of Hanslick and Gurney account in large measure for differences in their conclusions, although no commentator on their writings notes significant differences between the authors, either in methods or in conclusions. Hanslick's conclusion was either that there is no such thing as musical expression, or that musical expression is irrelevant in determining whether music is beautiful. Looking at his inquiry as scientific, and therefore one in search of necessary and sufficient conditions, Gurney, on the other hand, concluded that expression is neither a necessary nor a sufficient condition of what he alternately termed musical "impressiveness" or beauty. This, then, did not entail his denial that there is such a thing as musical expression, nor that *on occasion* expressiveness makes a relevant contribution to musical impressiveness. On the contrary, "the element of expression . . . may reach the very extreme of intensity and profundity, since the whole mass of musical feeling which is stirred up appears steeped in the color of any special emotion it may suggest. But it is subordinate (1) in the sense that it is far from being a constant element; (2) in the sense that not in it, but in the independently impressive aspect of Music, must be sought the explanation of the essential effect of the art; and that the very intensity of which musical expression is capable, so far from being explanatory, is one of the prime mysteries to be explained."[3]

Although both Hanslick and Gurney acknowledged the existence of a power in music which is primitive or primordial, and exclusive of expressive features, it was Gurney's method, not Hanslick's, which promised, if any could, to explain this. Indeed, Hanslick himself noted more than once that no psychology *could* explain it.[4] Much of Gurney's search centered on the influence of past auditory circumstances upon present auditory experiences. His observation about the "musical child" is characteristic. Hanslick, on the other hand, spoke with contempt of the "uninitiated" (p. 99) and his unabashed snobbery in favor of "the intellectual principle" (p. 50) moves clearly away from recognition of any significant commonality of musical understanding among men. "If people allow themselves to be so completely carried away by what is elemental in art as to lose all self-control, this scarcely redounds to the glory of the art, and much less to that of the individual" (p. 93).

Both Hanslick and Gurney have frequently been dubbed "musical purists." The term *purism,* however, should now be recognized as clearly and multiply ambiguous. Both Hanslick's and Gurney's versions of purism are consistently negative, are essentially *denials* of something. It seems, however, that any hope for dissolving the problem of musical purism as linguistic in origin must follow Hanslick's, not Gurney's, methodological lead. So far as Gurney's method is concerned, claims to have dissolved the problem will beg his question.

Central to Gurney's version of musical purism is his hypothesis of the "unique and isolated musical faculty." Although he claimed to have found some necessary conditions of musical "impressiveness," Gurney could find none that was sufficient, and so brought in the "musical faculty" to complete in a negative way an otherwise incomplete explanation. What has seemed so unsatisfactory about Gurney's posited sufficient condition is not only that "faculty psychology" in itself has long been suspect, nor even that, in the light of recent Wittgensteinian enlightenment, no one in aesthetic inquiries is looking for necessary and sufficient conditions anymore. A more primary question is how Gurney could seriously posit the existence of *anything* unique and isolated in a scientifically understood world.

"If I am right," wrote James Sully, "Mr. Gurney's hypothesis of a unique [musical] faculty is an unnecessary *deus ex machina.* . . . His argument looks very much like a fallacy of composition:— The charm of music is due neither to this, that, nor the other cause: therefore it is not due to all taken together."[5] In reply to his critic, Gurney did not deny that his theory of a unique musical faculty was a *deus ex machina.* But he did deny that such a theory was unnecessary.

> No look of notes on music paper, no analysis of structure, no computation of numerical relations, will establish any sort of condition or set of conditions applicable to combinations which present freedom and novelty, and not to others which present triteness and tameness of movement. . . . I take two melodies, A with charm, B without; and I say the charm of A is not due to order, for B is equally orderly; nor to suggestion of physical movement, for B bears just the same analogy to physical movement; nor to suggestion of speech, for B is just as suggestive (or unsuggestive) of speech: therefore it is not due to all taken together. What it *is* due to (primarily at any rate) is the fact that A presents one set of sound-proportions, and B another, to the single faculty which can judge of such matters; so that however much such a faculty may be a *deus ex machina,* it can hardly be deemed "unnecessary."[6]

Since the early twentieth century, we have been familiar with John Dewey's determined battle against all metaphysical and epistemological "dualisms." Musical purism, either of Hanslick's or of Gurney's brand, would be classic cases of philosophical "dualism." If any inquiry came out in defense of anything isolated, or probably in most cases also unique (one can think of each snowflake as unique, yet scientifically analyzable), such inquiry would have been consigned to the bin of classic philosophical errors. Yet we have in Gurney the same expectations of philosophy, the same correlation as we find in Dewey between theoretical or philosophical inquiries and psychology, between philosophy and science. Both writers would have denied Kant's distinction between "transcendental" philosophy and empirical psychology. But not only in broad outlines were the inquiries of Dewey and Gurney compatible. Subsidiary similarities between them are marked even down to the minutiae of psychological vocabulary. Both based aesthetic descriptions upon recognition of mutual dependence between observer and observed. Thus, the "form" of an art work was identified by both as a process of (in Dewey's terms) "interaction" between "organism and environment." Psychological functions understood to be involved in this process by Dewey and Gurney were the same or closely analogous, Gurney even anticipating vocabulary considered to be typical of early American psychology: habit, intelligence, expectation, satisfaction, interest, attention, desire, seeking, memory, recognition, association, comparison, and coordination.[7] Results of these functions were described by both authors as "fusions," rather than as collections of distinguishable parts. Both authors stressed the presence of something, in Dewey's terms "new," in Gurney's terms "unpredictable." Both authors made special note of value judgments as of the "immediate" or "direct." As Dewey found the mark of aesthetic value in *any* human experience in its "consummatory" phases, Gurney stressed in musical impressiveness a "triumphant justification of a sense of potential and coming integration."[8] In all of these ways, Gurney's theory could be considered just as antidualistic as Dewey's.

The source of the primary difference between these two authors' results appears to lie in Dewey's failure to draw distinctions in epistemological functions between visual, auditory, tactual, or other sensory media. Dewey's insistence that aesthetic experience, indeed that the core of great art, lay in the "everyday events, doings and sufferings" of universal human experience presupposed a norm of psychological function that bypassed domination of different sensory media in different individuals, and obscured the possibility that auditory perception in particular could yield information and value judgments about the world at variance in any crucial way with those common to all human experience. Gurney, on the other hand, began his book with a detailed attempt to differentiate between comparative significance of different senses. He singled out the eye and ear as "higher senses."

There is a fundamental peculiarity of the eye and ear which utterly differentiates them from the other sense-organs, and which sets them, as regards the scope of their activities and the enjoyment attainable through them, in a position totally apart. This peculiar-

ity is extreme delicacy and complexity—the possession by both
organs of a multitude of terminal elements *capable of separate
individual action* [italics added]. . . . It is owing to this that the
experiences are possible, which constitute these two senses beyond
all comparison our most important channels of communication
with the world of people and things, and place the impressions
received through them in a *wholly unique* [italics added] relation
to our intellectual and emotional activity.[9]

The source of Gurney's claim to a unique and isolated musical
faculty lay in his early and implicit recognition that auditory perception had a temporal priority over other sensory media. He
never got so far as to suggest that audition has priority in this
respect over vision, nor to trace auditory perception and its
influence to anything prenatal. But his method of explanation of
the "power of sound" was essentially a genetic one. His search
was for principles "beyond the choice and control of individuals"
(p. 26) and that were therefore neither "transient" nor "accidental"
(p. 13). Although his distinction between the "natural" and "arti-
ficial" was itself a dualism that Dewey abhorred, Gurney's iso-
lation of auditory perception for separate study—his question: Is
there information and/or enjoyment to be found through one
sense medium that is not to be found through others—is not in
itself incompatible with Dewey's method. Gurney's conclusions
concerning audition may appear to us suspect. The important
point is that he pursued this tack at all. The method of Hanslick,
or that of later language analysts, extends to the scholar no such
invitation. Within the method of analysis of language of music
critics, there is suggested no explanation of its typically and
spatially metaphorical character.

Gurney observed that the rudiments of sound that any hearing
individual finds "in nature" are either "unformed" noises or tones.
These are typically monotonous and neutral in character, lacking
in precision, regularity or complexity, disparate and transient (pp.
23-27). "The characteristics of non-musical sounds never strike us
as shades of some common character in reference to which they
can be compared. A cough is one thing, the sound of a waterfall
is another, the grating of a saw is another. The first may be
neutral, the second pleasant, the third unpleasant; they may
present varying degrees of suddenness or of loudness, and in
these respects we can certainly compare them; but in their lack of

any essential common nature, they are disparate things . . ."
(p. 27). It is perception of "form"—a process of combining and
coordinating "sets of elementary sense-impressions"—that conditions perception of beauty. Auditory perceptions do not generally form for us "groups" having the character of "objectivity and
permanence" such as we regularly find in things seen and that are
often "confirmed" through muscular and tactual observations that
yield "the most vivid sense of external contact and resistance"
(pp. 12, 13). When auditory perceptions are grouped and formed
and acquire an "objectivity and permanence," these are results of
human artifice, choice, and control.[10] There appears to be no
"external" condition guiding these groupings as there does in
formations through vision. Thus, "in the case of the ear . . . the
combination of sense impressions into coherent groups of any
complexity takes place *exceptionally,* but with a resulting beauty
often comparable in degree to the very best attained by visual
forms . . ." (p. 15). There is a "fundamental peculiarity presented
by the sense of hearing, in the very occasional character of that
highest activity which gives it its place in relation to Beauty, and
makes it equally with sight the key to an otherwise unimaginable
world" (p. 25).

     If, then, the source of Gurney's explanations of musical beauty
lies in human choices among auditory perceptions, the next step is
to ask on what ground the choices are made. Many of Gurney's
observations are related to connections that might be forged between auditory perceptions and visual/tactual perceptions of the
spatial world. Thus, he compared qualities of "force," "pace,"
"mass," and "rhythm" in music with those of spatially located
objects in motion. None yielded a sufficient condition of musical
beauty or "impressiveness." Again, he took special note of connections of music with human speech:

> A fine melody produces [the vivid effect] of being *something
> said*—a real *utterance* of transcendent significance. So prominent
> is this characteristic that the instinct to project some sort of per-
> sonality behind melodic strains seems absolutely irresistible. . . .
> [Again] two melodic parts may seem to sustain a dialogue or a
> dispute. . . . [Or] the suggested feeling which is perhaps best
> described as a *sense of multitude*, produced by vast masses of
> sonorous impression—especially in connection with actual delivery
> by a multitude, as in a great chorus—may involve true though

very vague and intangible social associations. . . . The list of affini-
ties between Music and speech could easily be extended. . . . Far
more important than the features themselves is the point that they
are quite undistinctive of what is musically essential; that one may
find them as readily in music that he cares nothing for as in music
that he loves; while none the less they contribute to give music
which is truely [sic] enjoyed that peculiar character of utterance,
as of a message from others, and now again so possessing us that
we seem to find its source in the deepest springs of our own
emotional nature.[11]

These last sentences mark the closest Gurney came to recognizing a power of musical sound properly described as both social
and solipsistic, a power appearing in the case of analogies with
speech to be based on expressive functions. Yet it was *as* expressive functions that he rejected them from his "generic explanations." Failing wherever he looked—either at formal musical
relations or at expressive or representative functions—he posited
a musical faculty as the needed condition that was both a constant
and a psychological premise governing individual choices among
auditory forms. In the end, the source of the power of musical
sound remained almost the mystery it was at the start. Like other
capacity-concepts—for example, that of "musical genius"—the
musical faculty was in essence a place-holder for Gurney and was,
as he himself admitted, "inscrutable."

If Gurney had had access to a playback of prenatal sounds,
he might have realised that there exist sounds "in nature" that are
not unformed, that there does exist a sound-rhythm complex
"beyond the choice and control of individuals." He might then
also finally have agreed with Sully that his hypothesis of a musical
faculty was unnecessary. But his conviction that there is a condition of the power of sound that is "unique" and "isolated" would
stand. Surely prenatal sounds are isolated from anything known
through visual/tactual perception of the spatial world, and in that
fact they are also unique. Herein, it seems, lies the Achilles' heel of
Dewey's antidualism. The suggestions of the last chapter appear
to be closer to the old "wax tablet" theory of mind, and also to
Plato's doctrine of recollection, than they do to Dewey's naturalistic account of human experience within the challenges of the
space-time world.

Plato's doctrine, of course, was of recollection of Ideas or

Forms free of sense perception altogether, and the "wax tablet" theory of mind is too crude a theory for twentieth-century science. Nonetheless, the suggestion of both is of mind as a passive recipient of knowledge, rather than as an active participant or agent in producing it. It appears to be the posited forming *activity* of the mind that gave Gurney trouble in defining the musical faculty. He thought of the musical faculty, after all, as a choice-making *function*. That, he found to be inscrutable. Looking now at what might be termed prenatal auditory conditioning, we may be tempted to think in gross contemporary terms of brainwashing, or of neurological coding, such that musical forms that are clearly reminiscent of very early auditory experiences will predictably be favored over those which are not so reminiscent. If thought of in these terms, this would not be a result of any person's conscious intent to direct or persuade us. It would simply be a result of the way human beings come "packaged." It would be, as Gurney put it, "in nature."

From our analysis of depth metaphor in music criticism, Gurney appears to have been right in positing a major condition of musical power that is unique and isolated. This result, as is ours, was based on an empirical and genetic method which analyzed auditory perception independently of visual/tactual perception. It should not be forgotten, however, that we made no claim in chapter one to having found a sufficient condition for depth judgments of musical works, such that an obvious or close analogue of prenatal sounds will guarantee a judgment of depth. Neither have we been clear about how far an auditory analogue can differ from these sounds and still possibly trigger some recall— albeit probably a radically transformed one. In our analogy with Proust's recall, we have not asked whether it might have been possible for Proust to recall Sunday mornings in Combray as vividly—or indeed to recall them at all—if he had tasted pound-cake dipped in tea, instead of a madeleine. Similarly, we have made no attempt to pin down auditory analogues so precisely as to allow us to say, for example, that analogues of "diastolic sounds," translatable into Eb-Db, can explain why these tones may "move us to the depths" in one context and not in another, nor to ask specifically how deviant from an exact whole-tone drop such tones can be and still be possibly effective analogues for recall. Most important to bear in mind is that the primary critical criterion we have been concerned with—and what Gurney seems mainly to have been searching for—is not the only criterion by which we judge music as having maximum aesthetic value. There is also, almost as a constant companion for Western Europeans, the criterion of "greatness." In musical greatness, as in musical depth, we have a criterion that is always valuationally positive to the maximum degree. For greatness, however, we appear to need a certain size and a certain complexity that are not needed for depth. A deep composition *may* be large and complex, but it need not be. Whereas Gurney's genetic method was more clearly in search of the "elemental" power of music, in his stress on the "intellectual principle" and "form," Hanslick appeared more clearly to be pursuing conditions of greatness. In point of method, Hanslick's logical and linguistic analyses may well be more suitable than Gurney's empirical observations on auditory perception for explicating a quality found in tonal and rhythmic forms having considerable size and complexity.

A pursuit-of-greatness criteria, however, promises little or no explanation of persistent claims to universality of musical understanding among men, claims that music transcends cultural differences in tone and rhythm organization, or that it unites men in a common humanity. It also ties aesthetic inquiry closely to Western European musical composition of the past approximately two hundred fifty years. Inquiries into origins of great music remain compatible with an *active* notion of the composer's mind, almost blinding us to a possibility that a *passive* mind may be the one that finds major aesthetic value in auditory art. They cannot make much sense of Hegel's observation about musical talent: "Musical talent declares itself as a rule in very early youth, when the head is still empty and the emotions have barely had a flutter; it has, in fact, attained real distinction at a time in the artist's life when both intelligence and life are practically without experience."[12]

Probably the most important point in favor of Gurney's method over Hanslick's, however, lies in its suggestion that there is another source of aesthetic value in musical sound besides "form" or "expressiveness" of particular compositions. If Bach's and Mozart's compositions are great, we are tempted to look into Bach's architectonic forms or into Mozart's expressiveness for explanations. Patient, logical analysis of the concepts of "expression" and "form" is then indeed in order. But if a simple little tune "moves us to the depths"—in that certain *turn* which is just right, perhaps bringing tears—its "depth" is not expressed and its form is so simple as to defy analysis. If our only routes to explanation remain Hanslick's—either essentially logical analyses of expression or of form—we shall forever be frustrated. We must, it seems, move out of logical or linguistic analyses into speculative psychology and deny, as both Gurney and Dewey did, the Kantian separation of logical and empirical inquiry. Put another way, we must acknowledge that language analysis cannot completely explicate metaphor that relates to or derives in part from a prelinguistic state where subject and predicate cannot be distinguished—a state that, contrary to common assumption, is not devoid of all sense perception whatsoever, but rather is devoid of the visual perception that seems to be our main source of knowing our subject-object world and of framing language through which we can talk nonmetaphorically about it—the world of numerical identities.

NOTES

1. *Aesthetics: Problems in the Philosophy of Criticism* (New York: Harcourt Brace and Co., Inc., 1958), 363.

2. *The Power of Sound* (London: Smith, Elder & Co., 1880), 368.

3. Ibid., 338.

4. *The Beautiful in Music* (New York: Bobbs-Merrill, 1957), 15, 51, 54, 58, 79, 83.

5. *Mind* 6 (1881):277.

6. *Mind* 7 (1882):92, 96, 97.

7. *The Power of Sound,* op. cit., especially 47, 51, 54, 63, 67, 68, 97, 157, 199, 204, 304, 308, 517.

8. Ibid., 166.

9. Ibid., 10.

10. Compare with Ingarden's identification of the musical work as a "purely intentional object." See *The Work of Music and the Problem of Its Identity,* translated by Adam Czerniawski, edited by Jean G. Harrell (Berkeley: University of California Press, 1986).

11. Ibid., 125, 364, 365, 373, 374 (n.1), 497.

12. G. W. F. Hegel, *The Philosophy of Fine Art,* translated by F. P. B. Osmaston (New York: Hacker Art Books, 1975), I, 37.

Three

Film Music:
Expression and Shallowness*

Our analysis of depth in music is incompatible in more than one way with common assumptions about depth in other arts. Not only does it trace depth in music to the most elemental of human conditions; it also takes depth to be a quality deriving from a passive mental function. Where depth is found in visual arts or in literature, indeed, where it is found as an aesthetic quality of philosophy itself, the quality is linked with profundity in wisdom, in a way that depth in music—at least as we have analyzed it—is not. In his discussion of Picasso's *Guernica,* Rudolf Arnheim expresses this well:

> The cult of the "unconscious" in creativity is an aspect of the danger of confusing the elementary with the profound. Cultures in their late stages develop an appetite for primitivism, and to satisfy it they endeavor to see in works of art the crudity of instincts or archetypes dressed up with the trimmings of civilization. But there is no reason to believe that the areas of the mind farthest from consciousness harbor the deepest wisdom. Wisdom can result only from the concerted effort of all the layers and capacities of the mind, and the prototype of art is not the stone colossus of the Easter Islands but the union of elementarity and subtlety found on the walls of Lescaux, through the ages, and in the canvases of Cézanne or the figures of Henry Moore. Although Picasso's *Guernica*—like every human product—has primitive roots, the picture is not a manifestation of primitivity.[1]

---

* This chapter is essentially an adaptation of the author's observations in "Phenomenology of Film Music," *Journal of Value Inquiry,* 14 (1980):23-34.

Such an understanding of depth or profundity as Arnheim's does not clearly distinguish the quality from a "manifestation" or an expression. In our own analogy with Proust's recall, however, we have not regarded the taste of a madeleine dipped in tea to be a manifestation of the look of Combray. Similarly, we have not regarded an auditory analogue in music to be a manifestation or an expression of prenatal sounds. Moreover, Arnheim's understanding of depth in visual art as a result of "concerted effort of all the layers and capacities of the mind" does not explain how *musical* depth may emerge from the hand of one whose "head is still empty," as Hegel put it, and whose "emotions have barely had a flutter." Our understanding of the rooting of musical depth in prenatal auditory experience may not be popular—or even heretofore thought of—but it has on this score better explanatory power.

In attempts to understand artistic depth, however, we should in fairness look for counterexamples. None appears more challenging than those to be found in that phenomenon peculiar to the twentieth century, the synchronized soundtrack of motion pictures. Unlike opera, where the primary art is music, in most film music, the visual has clear priority over the auditory. Often to a required split-second accuracy, film music is literally *endowed* with spatial location. Perhaps in this unique situation we can finally bring music under an umbrella—at least with the arts that make up cinema—and thus find significant challenge to our different understanding of a primary source of musical power. From its connection with visual art and literature, we should hope from Arnheim's view to find significant upgrading of depth-judgments of music in film. Yet this is precisely what we do *not* find. The metaphor typically applied to film music is the contrary metaphor of depth, i.e., *shallowness*. The persistent conviction remains among many that primary aesthetic value of musical art is *sui generis*, that it is not dependent upon any visual circumstances, or even upon the depth of literary themes. Tony Thomas recounts an attempt of Irving Thalberg to get Arnold Schoenberg to write the score for *The Good Earth* that seems to reflect this:

> In 1937, Thalberg asked Schoenberg to come to MGM to discuss the possibility of scoring *The Good Earth*. He was told by the producer that this film version of the Pearl Buck book was one of the studio's most artistic efforts and presented a rare opportunity

for a composer. Thalberg described one scene: "There's a terrific storm going on—the wheat fields are swaying in the wind, and suddenly the earth begins to tremble. Then, in the earthquake, the girl gives birth to a baby. What an opportunity for music." Schoenberg looked at him incredulously, "With so much going on, what do you need music for?" Thalberg was puzzled by this apparent lack of interest. He then asked Schoenberg, "What would be your terms in working for us?" Replied the composer, "I will write music and then you will make a motion picture to correspond with it." Neither Thalberg nor any other producer approached Schoenberg again.[2]

Perhaps, then, we can find an increase in, or at least a complement to depth-quality in music already composed, when it is juxtaposed against picture or story. Yet in the few attempts at this—most notably by Leopold Stokowski in the production of *Fantasia*—we do not find it. This is not to say that the synchronizations are not in any sense aesthetically successful. In 1941, Slavko Vorkapich, with his associate John Hoffman as collaborator, made a film titled *Moods of the Sea,* juxtaposing moving photography with Mendelssohn's *Fingal's Cave* overture. (This film was shot on the Pacific coast, but was presumably of the Hebrides.) Vorkapich was surely aware of Mendelssohn's letter to his sister, Clara, about his Hebrides voyage, in which he described how the musical phrase that seems to denote wave-shapes came to him. Clearly, however, Vorkapich's task was not simply to make a note-by-note, frame-by-frame correspondence. We find photographic symmetry with phrases typical of that genre of music, as well as the "clear and sharp contours of the melodies, the contrasts of tempos, dynamics, the surge and the quiescence, confluences between climaxes intended to connote the crash of waves and images of the waves themselves."[3] It appears, however, that Vorkapich's and Stokowski's attempts were primarily to force *expressive* functions of particular compositions through moving visual perceptions. Yet these juxtapositions, interesting and unusual as they might be, did not apparently increase or intensify any quality of depth that the compositions might independently have had. Indeed, we might argue that we have here some explanation for judgments that such juxtapositions with visual imagery "cheapen" the original music, at least where its significance does not derive from programmatic content.

That there is no intrinsic dependency of musical depth upon audio-visual expression is most evident in cases where film music has proven to be expressively powerful—sometimes too powerful—yet remains *musically* shallow. Consider an example recalled by David Raksin about the film version of Theodore Dreiser's novel, *Carrie* (1952):

> Carrie has left Hurstwood (Laurence Olivier) and goes her own way to fulfillment. Your re-introduction to Hurstwood—in the original print of the film—takes place in a horrid turn-of-the-century New York flophouse. We had a [long, high camera crane shot] through the flophouse—all you hear are sounds of men who have awoken drunk, coughing, retching, spitting. The camera moves into this tiny cubicle in which you see this wreck of a man who was once so beautiful. Director William Wyler said he wanted the music for this scene to be "towering." I said, "Willie, there's nothing I can do to approach the image you have on camera, and you know damn well that if I did, you'd have to squeeze the music down in order to hear all this coughing and spitting. What I have to do is think of something very meager. I don't know what but give me a little time." Well, I thought about it and came up with an idea: when you first saw Hurstwood he was the manager of a swank restaurant in Chicago and looked stunning in his morning coat and striped trousers. You saw him through Carrie's eyes and he was a sort of demi-God. Off screen there was a little orchestra playing a period waltz. I used this waltz as an association for Hurstwood and it made certain transformations in the film. Now I took a celesta and had them tape the bars, so that it would sound like a doll's piano. I played the waltz on this thing in a halting way, as a child would. The notes were dull and non-reverberating. It meant little when we recorded it but when we put it in the film the effect was absolutely hair-raising—all of a sudden you felt as if your skin was crawling. Everyone thought it was a "tour de force." But the producers decided the scene was too harrowing and the whole thing was cut.[4]

The source of the too-powerful expression of the "doll's piano" rendition of this music would be very hard to trace, and one would need to have seen the entire film to experience anything "hair-raising." *In context* it might be a reminder of childhood where delight reigns, yet the dull, non-reverberating tones of the taped celesta might distantly relate to premature death, thus to a denial of dynamic fullness of early life. However this might be, at the same time no one would describe *any* theme haltingly played by a child on a doll's piano as "deep music."

How can such a discrepancy between powerful expression and musical depth obtain? Surely our current and past philosophers have not so much as suggested an answer. In their primary concern with problems of expression, they have failed even to mention film music, consistently giving musical examples from the works of "the masters." Let it not be assumed, however, that composers of film music are simply weak composers and that this is why their work is overlooked by our aestheticians. Many strong composers have written for film, or at least have tried a hand at it. Criticism, rather, should be directed at those who have overlooked a veritable twentieth-century goldmine of expressive musical possibilities. In the overlooking, a fundamental difference between musical expression and quality of depth has been totally obscured. Depth and expression are frequently mixed in the work of the masters, such that citing the latter often may be confused with citing the former. But the quality of depth is *not* an expressed quality, and there appears to be something more fundamentally problematic about juxtaposing music with moving pictures other than that particular composers who happen to have tried this medium may be weak. To say so would be the weasel's way out. Our tracing of musical depth in chapter one to auditory experience prior to any visual perception suggests an explanation of the possible discrepancy between powerful expression and musical depth in cinema.

The primary point of cinema, after all, is visual access. If we do not have visual images before us, we do not have cinema, whatever else we may have of other scattered arts. Now a metaphor draws a likeness, but leaves a difference. If depth metaphor in music criticism draws a relation between what is aspatial and known by audition and what is spatially located but not visually accessible—what is *hidden* from view—then the attribution of depth to music synchronized with immediate, visual images should fail. And, in fact, it does fail. The likeness drawn by the metaphor is lost. What in criticism we consistently find is the contrary metaphor, *shallow*. Perhaps most interesting is the realization that *shallow* carries as consistently a negative judgment as *depth* carries a positive one. In this way, there is built into critical judgment of film music a negative evaluation.

Now, consider the role music has had in films of Shakespeare's plays, where we find borne out in *literary* depth the sort of profundity rooted in wisdom that Arnheim defines. Once more, we do not find praise of musical scores for their independent depth. In his criticism of Sir Laurence Olivier's production of *Hamlet*, Jack J. Jorgens finds:

> Although there are rare moments, like the combination of a beating heart and a moan as the ghost appears, [Olivier] relies primarily upon an orchestral score by William Walton . . . [that] bridges scenes, establishes moods, and identifies characters. Quite properly it is seldom realistic, and occasionally, as in the play scene, where the music is an analogue for Claudius's passion (it builds, he fights it down, and finally it erupts), blending suspense music with a repetitive, strangely sinister dance tune, it has real dramatic power. But on the whole, the sheer *ordinariness* of the music takes the edge off the performances and the language. There is nothing haunting, grand, or unpredictable about it. Often the hyperbolic clashes of cymbals, the repeated rushes up scales as the camera sweeps up to the ramparts, or the attempts to "point" speeches like "To be or not to be" come perilously close to unintentional humor.[5]

One may or may not agree with Jorgens's assessment of Walton's score for this film version of *Hamlet;* however, one may well wonder whether, if the music *had* been "haunting, grand, and unpredictable" throughout the film or had consistently "real dramatic power," it would have controverted a play whose literary depth clearly does not depend upon any musical score. Although Jorgens criticizes Olivier's use of sound as "less inventive" than his relating of visual effects to "physical movements and to the rhythms and meanings of the lines,"[6] we might wonder whether correlations of visual effects with literary meaning may be more generally suitable and compatible with Shakespeare's literary depth than correlations of music ever can be. Olivier clearly capitalized upon visual possibilities through the camera that could not be duplicated on the stage, yet which poignantly complemented passages in this play of consummate literary depth. Where, for example, Hamlet has died and Horatio speaks his famous lines "Good night, sweet prince, And flights of angels sing thee to thy rest!," the camera moves slowly around Hamlet's head in close-up, like a parent's caressing hand, coming to rest on the crown of his hair. One can hardly think of any use of music at this point that could match or intensify the poignancy and pain of this moment, nor any music that, through its connection with such pain, could itself gain in musical depth. On this point, note should be made also of Peter Brook's 1970 film version of *King Lear*, which is without any music at all.

Real question can be raised about compatibility of music with literary depth found independently of any cinematic images at all.* Consider Schubert's musical setting of Göethe's poem *Der Erlkönig*. Here again, we have literature trafficking with universal and consummate human pain, in a portrayal to an adult of the death of a child—not only this, but of a child who knows that he is dying and is dying in terror. Here, Göethe reaches a point in literature that one would almost call "unbearable," that would almost cause one to turn away, as from Eisenstein's scenes of the murdering of children and mothers in *Battleship Potemkin* and *Alexander Nevsky*. In Schubert's setting, one may find many compatibilities with Göethe's poem. The wild ride of the father and son through the night, the mirroring of beat of the German language and of the horse's hooves, the anxiety of the father, determined to console and calm his son, the son's rising terror, the sweet-talk of the Erlking—all this and more could be said to be complemented or reinforced by Schubert's setting, aided, of course, by the particular rendition of the singer. But all of these can be considered aspects of what might be called the "thriller-chiller" level of the poem. There is nothing in Schubert's setting of the poem that is properly called almost "unbearable."

The last word of the poem, *tot*, is final in at least three ways: least significant, it is the last word of the poem. Next, it answers the question of the poem: the child was dead. *Tot* also names a condition that is absolutely final. Nothing is more final than death, but it is a finality that is wrong. Nobody wants it. People build temples, give alms, say prayers to get out of it. If one were to say that the V-I cadence of Schubert following this word also is final,

---

* Consideration of a possible fundamental source of discrepancy between musical depth and depth of tragedy will be made in chapter four.

it is a finality that, musically speaking, is absolutely right. The circular direction of the music fights the linear direction of the poem, and returning the listener as it does to the beginning of the musical setting, wraps the poem up in what seems finally more musically right than conceptually wrong and painful. Yet within Schubert's system of musical composition it seems difficult to see how he could have avoided this, no matter what his talent, no matter what his inspiration. Schubert *might* have ended his setting on the "plagal" or "Amen" cadence, that is, on IV-I. But not only would this have controverted the clearly V-I harmonic structure of the entire composition, it would also have added a lugubrious quality to the ending, again casting a superficial significance upon the poem's depth.

The question of relation of musical depth to literary depth may connect with Aristotle's thinking on sources of effective tragedy. For Aristotle, the power and "nobility" of tragedy did not depend only upon the "necessity" and "probability" of sequences in plot. The tragic impact also depended upon characters going "from good fortune to bad." Our analysis of musical depth relates it intimately to recall (unconscious) of dynamic, vigorous life, prior to the challenges and pains and dangers in the spatial world. To the extent that literary depth often, perhaps characteristically, traffics with human misfortunes culminating in death, as well as in things beneficial to life, in these most fundamental concerns—life and death—we have some explanation of apparent incompatibility of depth-quality when it is found in music and when it is found in literature, or for that matter in painting, sculpture, or the visual aspects of cinema. Where we try to think of counterexamples, for example, Chopin's "Funeral March" (*Sonata #2* in Bb minor, third movement, Op. 35), a composition that has been related to death in the most rudimentary way, qualities—alternately of empty desolation and of the light of life regained—appear to be qualities expressed. Were the "Funeral March" not clearly connected through its use and associations with the basic human tragedy of death, one wonders whether, independently of these, the first lugubrious section (and one to which the composition returns) might not consistently be regarded simply as a dragging musical composition.

One of the most commonly noted examples in a Shakespeare film, one where music has been taken to function most effectively, is William Walton's music for the Battle of Agincourt in *Henry V*. Yet, although we may say that the musical score in this case "makes" the scene, its triumph is not one of having separate musical depth.

> For sheer excitement—excitement that provoked the sophisticated Press-showing audience to an ovation—the crescendo of the French cavalry charge which commenced the Battle of Agincourt would be hard to surpass. I suspect the audience did not realize that they were applauding "t'other side"—but no matter. The gathering momentum of the charge was enhanced by the cunningly mixed sound-track. A long "cross-fade" brought the music to the foreground, interchanging in prominence with the harness and armor-clanking sound effects as the charge gathered its impetus. The director very wisely suppressed the effects and allowed the music its full head as the climax approached. The result was a tour-de-force which, with the action and strident primary colors of the banners and the surcoats of the knights, drew a burst of spontaneous applause from the audience.[7]

The Battle of Agincourt was a single sequence, and the success of the musical score at this point was limited to it. Typically, judgments of music in film are of this limiting sort. Jorgens's assessment of Walton's score for *Hamlet* was in its bridging of scenes, establishing of moods, and identification of characters. Again, Walton himself noted: "The value to a film of its musical score rests chiefly in the creation of mood, atmosphere, and the sense of period. When the enormous task of reimagining a Shakespearean drama in terms of the screen has been achieved, these three qualities, which must be common to all film music, appear in high relief."[8]

Ingmar Bergman's use of music in films whose themes are as deep and disturbing as any can be—for example, infidelity in *Scenes from A Marriage*, sibling death in *Cries and Whispers*, and mental breakdown in *Face to Face*—is spare, almost not there at all. Consistently, fragments from well-known compositions are used, and from compositions that are themselves independently noticeable, that tempt attraction to themselves alone. But, within context, Bergman does not let them get that far. They seem to be picked for suitability to the time and place, as Chopin is used in the turn-of-the-century piece, *Cries and Whispers,* or for qualities consonant with emotional condition of the characters, as in the use of Mozart in *Face to Face*. In such use of compositions that independently have their own musical depth, in their fragmented state and secondary role in film we seem only to find a reinforcing of a literary depth that is established quite independently of them. In other ways, we repeatedly find judgment of music in film in the kinds of limited capacity here considered. Actors have often noted how, in some particular scene, the music helped the final result. Edward G. Robinson is quoted, commenting on Bronislau Kaper's score for a particular scene from *The Stranger:* "My acting became so much better after they added the music." George Peppard is quoted, again commenting on Kaper's music: "There's a long scene in *Home from the Hill* where the camera stays on me as I walk to a cemetery. People are always saying what a fine piece of acting it was. Actually, I didn't do anything but walk and stare ahead. All the acting was done by Kaper."[9]

Such comments need not only refer to emotional expression of the music. Music may distinctly influence timing and rhythm of action, or speed of a particular visual sequence. In Christian Blackwood's documentary, *Hollywood's Musical Moods* (1975), Miklos Rozsa quotes a scene from *Spellbound,* first with music, then without. In this scene, the camera focuses on a series of objects—a basin, a chair, a doorway. Without sound, the camera shots appear in rapid sequence, and one may wonder, in context, why the cameraman shot so many views so fast. Rosza's variation of the film's theme on the theremin (a melodic electronic instrument) apparently slows down the speed of visual sequence, and greatly enhances its significance.

Perhaps, then, when we are looking for an increase in depth of a musical dimension in film, we should look to a musical influence over the *entire* film, rather than to fragmentary functions in particular sequences. In this, there appear to be two primary features of film music, neither of which is expressive. The first is a *unifying* function. The second may be found in a kind of *double entendre* established between the "external" world of the audience and the (often) fictional world of the film.

In considering the unifying function that music may have in a film, a distinction first needs to be drawn between this sense of *unify* and the more usual sense that Aristotle had in mind in tracing "organic unity" in tragedy to a certain kind of plot. Indeed, we may posit in the "nobility" of tragedy that literary depth is presupposed. At least, for the sake of argument, let us assume that there is a connection with Aristotle's vocabulary. Rather than emerging through logically "necessary" or "probable" sequences of plot, however, a unifying function of film music appears to occur through the exercise of auditory memory. The sense of unity provided in film scores seems to come through *memory,* through temporal rather than logical unity, in which past and present events are brought together as though no time had elapsed, as Proust's madeleine dipped in tea brought back the immediacy of years long past. This kind of unity seems to result from a time-telescoping or eclipsing rather than from logical connections between episodes, and it may appear as a chief means of unifying episodic plots. Indeed, it may provide what-ever semblance of depth an otherwise shallow film may contain.

In Aristotle's opinion, the weakest candidate for effective tragic plot was the episodic plot, such as is found in historical narratives. One of the most prominent episodic plots in recent literature is that of Margaret Mitchell's *Gone With the Wind.* The book's critics still reflect a certain Aristotelian intellectual snobbishness. Long as the novel was, readers could not bear to have it end, and so wrote to the author, asking: "What happened next?" (A similar attitude is taken toward television watchers who attend to anything and everything, regardless of whether a smidgen of logic is required to bring it all together.) The "Tara" theme of Max Steiner for the film version of *Gone With the Wind* (1939) seems to provide this film with its primary sense of unity. In fact, it seems to yield a film story better unified than that of the novel, although the fact that much of the novel was cut may also have been a contributing factor.

Initially, the theme is a *leitmotif* for a place, Tara, and sounds only when action takes place there or when Tara is mentioned in the dialogue. Yet in spite of this, and in spite of the fact that the score contains sixteen main themes and almost three hundred separate musical segments,[10] the "Tara" theme is the one identified with the entire film, sounding at its beginning, again at its end, and prominent enough in the interim to tie events together. Admittedly, this is not a logical process, but it *is* a form of remembering. Steiner's use of this theme is not a case of simple repetition, and is marked by what seems to have been a favorite method of his: When things in the story go wrong, the same theme or fragments of it reappear, but are thrown out of harmonic whack. This was the way of connection when Scarlett O'Hara finally reached Tara again and found it in ruins, her mother dead, her father insane. This again was the connection in using "Dixie" for the scene of Atlanta's streets filled with wounded and dying soldiers, the camera high above, giving the sweeping view. The strength of tie-in or carry-over of the "Tara" theme seems such as to allow the audience an intermission, to leave the auditorium, and still be sufficiently undistracted to return to the second part of the film and almost immediately, through this theme, to connect it with the opening of the first. Itself independently attractive, the theme, in its pervasiveness, also throws a romantic, nostalgic aura over the entire production.

Even in plots that are not episodic, music may be a chief means to unify a film story. In *Une Partie du Plaisir* (1975), Claude Chabrol uses fragments from compositions of Beethoven, Brahms, and Schumann. A fragment may be repeated two or three times, ending just at a point of resolution. Although several scenes may follow with no music at all, when music finally returns, the resolution of the previous fragment is heard, thus tying the succession of scenes together musically. Again, the treatment of the theme for *Laura* (1944) appears as a chief unifying factor of a story that seems independently to break in two. The first part of the story is primarily concerned with detailing the qualities of Laura, presumably to heighten the question: "Why would anyone want to kill her?" The second part is concerned exclusively with identifying the murderer. There is a kind of coda, after the murderer has been identified, in the question: "Is he now going to kill Laura, after all?" This seems to create a very awkward point at which to end the story. The last scene, in which the murderer is shot and dying, would almost cause the story to fall flat, were it not for the independently strong music that picks it up, cuts it off, as much as to say "That's *it!*" We seem to get at the end, through the music, a summing commentary: "Now *that* was a story, eh?" The time-telescoping produces a film that seems to be quite short. All, or almost all, of the music for *Laura* derives from the theme, but again the use of the theme throughout the movie is far from a case of simple repetition. Primary variations are effected in instrumentation, speed of rendition, and theme fragmentation.

In an article on Sir Laurence Olivier's film, *Richard III*, Jack Diether notes that Olivier has described himself as an "illustrator" of Shakespeare, rather than as a literal transcriber on film of the original plays. Diether comments:

> Using about half of the total number of lines of the play (*Richard III*), adding a few from *Henry V*, Part 3, and other sources, and scrambling them thoroughly in respect to syntax and order of presentation, Olivier has fashioned a film in which the basic ingredients of plot are . . . both simplified and clarified . . . The plain fact is that Olivier's method [enforces] quality between the aural demands of Shakespeare's poetry and the visual demands of the movie camera, with music as an important third factor. . . . The film is thoroughly unified and integrated on its own terms, and brilliantly presented—on those terms.

Diether gives several detailed examples of ways in which he finds that William Walton's score contributes to the "unity" of this film and concludes: "Since it is within the province of music to augment quite unconsciously in the minds of the spectators the structural unity Shakespeare always strove for, Olivier is quite justified in giving it a leading part."[11] From his analysis, we might say that in Diether's implicit opinion, Walton's score for *Richard III* partakes of visual/literary depth, although in recorded, "concertized" versions of the music separated from the film, the result may be quite different. Indeed, it seems that it is unifying functions of music in film that bring it closest to our understanding of musical depth found independently of any visual perception, and independently of any expressive functions which the music may have.

All of these examples of unifying function of music in film are clearly dependent upon auditory memory. They capitalize upon a source of aesthetic value that Proust found in memory of long ago, but are established in an immediate time frame, within a few hours at best, and are contingent upon particular story and photographic circumstances. Thus, rather than leading the listener to film music (by our interpretation) to find something "primordial" and "deep" that he "can't put his finger on," in *historical* films he is led to a state of nostalgia for what he identifies quite clearly, i.e., "the good old days." Audiences do not seem generally to realize that the source of aesthetic value, the nostalgia that they find in some films, derives from a time-telescoping function of a musical score. One may well wonder how flat or interminably long the film production of *Gone With the Wind* would have been without any musical score at all, or whether *Laura* would have become the favored mystery film it has become without David Raksin's music.

There is, however, a primary point to note about any music in film, whether it functions to unify or does not. Presumably, depth in art is found in its connections with the real world. Abstract logic, for example, is seldom, if ever, called deep. In philosophy, it is rather metaphysics that is consistently called deep. The addition of music to cinema, however, makes cinema to that extent unreal. In the real world people and events do not have *leitmotifs,* nor in other ways is music glued onto them. (The closest you could come to an exception would be the blond beachboy with his everpresent transistor blaring the music that "goes" with him.)

To the extent that nostalgia for the *good* old days is established by a film's musical soundtrack, to that extent it is not for the *real* old days. Of course, in the real world, people attach music to certain specific objects or events. But this connection is accidental. "Our song" is just the one that happened to be being played when "We" met and the sparks started flying. And if what happened to have sounded was a Bach fugue, the incongruity might have been such that the music would have been ignored, and "We" would not have had a Song at all. Muzak is everywhere—in the elevator, the restaurant, the dentist's office. But even when he is playing something lovely and you pay attention, you could be looking at anything or doing anything and it wouldn't matter. Consider the criticism that would probably be levelled against a newscaster who decided to add music to his film of, say, fighting in Lebanon. He would probably be accused of inaccurate, even of prejudicial reporting, on the ground that the music was not a part of the real fighting. Addition of music to real events may endow them with an aura, a feeling quality, even a moral attitude that, in "objective" reporting, appear gratuitous. Although the story of *The Godfather* was based on fact, Nino Rota's main theme in the film version (1972), sounding first in desolate trumpet solo, seemed to function like a moral commentator, telling the audience: "*Look* at this! Walk with me through these streets, these doors, these halls. *Look* at these people who cannot see their own moral desolation. *Look* at this moral wasteland!"

Music, glued to a particular film, can carry beyond it. As an audience carries its sounds, fading in the mind's ear, out of the theater, into the harsh light and sounds of the real world, it can infuse its lingering romance into a simple act of feeding a parking meter. (That meter might never have been fed in quite that way before, perhaps with a flamboyance and curl of the little finger that would startle the passerby.) But it cannot last. It may be that film-track recordings sell and become popular precisely in an attempt to *make* it last. But it seems that if the music becomes independently popular, it loses its singular connection with the particular film. It comes unglued. In cases where a musical theme is later set to words to make a song, its function simply changes. For example, the theme for *Laura* was *with* Laura and a lot of other things in the film; when it was later set to words, it became more nearly *about* her.

People are concerned that youth, fed a constant diet of violence in movies, will lose the ability to differentiate between the play world and the real world, and go out and do the evil deeds in the street that they see in the theater. Violence in film, though, nearly always is accompanied by music, and by music that itself may be violent. It is this musical dimension of the deed that helps make it *right*—not in the sense of morally right, but in the ontological sense of the way it *is*. (This seems to carry in phrases about music such as "With it" and "Where it's *at*.") It makes sense to think that the evil deed, done in the real world without its musical dimension, would strike anyone (except perhaps the tone-deaf person) as wrong, as a kind of misfiring.

Still, where music in film has consistently accompanied certain character or situation types, these may in some circumstances appear the more real for their musical dimension. When children play cowboys and Indians and sing along their own soundtracks, they appear to view their antics, to be complete, as requiring a musical dimension. Where television commercials for a certain perfume or washday detergent are always accompanied by the same identifiable themes, that musical dimension that helps make them the right ones to buy may sorely be missed when the consumer sees in the department store only a bald little bottle on some glass shelf without any lady on a white horse, dressed in gauze, dashing through a swamp and that certain music; or when that detergent box with all the right colors now appears stacked on a supermarket shelf at the wrong hour without that image of whiter-than-white wash against a blue sky and that certain music. One may well wonder whether Charles Manson and Bobby Beausoleil,* in doing or even thinking about their evil deeds, provided themselves with some soundtrack—if only in their minds' ears—as children do when they play cowboys and Indians. Such constancies, however, would only have been produced since the advent of the synchronized soundtrack, and in musical respects their "reality" remains bracketed.

Sometimes a more subtle, or at least more complicated connection may be found between film music and the real world, in a kind of double-entendre. The source of music in some films may be photographed, heard by the characters, indeed sometimes made by them, yet have a different significance to them from what it has to the audience. In this way what appears disconnected from reality in the fictional film world also may connect with the real world of the audience. Because of such transfer from the unreal film world to the real world of the audience, claim may be made for a depth—or at least a universality—of the particular film. Although what is heard is interpreted as a part of the unreal film world, its different significance to the audience may seem to give it a universal human significance that is not found in the film's immediate circumstances.

In an early scene of *The Picture of Dorian Gray* (1945), as Dorian Gray walks along a street he is arrested by the sounds of Chopin's D minor Prelude (Opus 28, no. 24), wildly interpreted on a distant piano. He is strongly attracted to this music and seeks it out, climbing a long flight of stairs to a garret door. Flinging the door open, he confronts a white-headed old man seated at a piano. "Does that have a *name?*," he asks. "It has a kind of name," the old man replies. "It's called Prelude." The age, white hair, the speech of the man (all symbolizing wisdom to a point of cliché,) are prophetic to the audience—as is the very name of the composition—in a way that probably neither the old man nor Dorian

---

* An organist and composer of considerable ability (who is also insane), Beausoleil has written scores for at least three films that have not been released.

Gray themselves understand. In the film the old man's presence seems necesssary mainly to render the prelude, and Dorian Gray's disturbance by it may suggest that his deception won't succeed, yet this remains unclear. As the prelude is repeated through the film, its prophetic quality increases. Dorian Gray is not going to get away with selling his soul for youth forever. The significance of the prelude in this context seems to carry, no matter what previous acquaintance the audience may have had with Chopin's music.

In a more intricate and subtle way, David Raksin's theme for *Laura* comes out in layers. Initially, the audience is introduced to it before the first scene, presumably as a theme for the whole movie; the rendition is strong and vigorous, is in popular idiom, and gives a clue to the kind of story it complements. Soon into the first phase of the story, the detective is seen in Laura's apartment with others who comment about her. A snatch of a favorite recording is played on her phonograph. Among other things, she had good taste—not "exactly Classical"—but good. It is evident that this theme is known publicly in the world of these people (stressed by the interpretation in the recording of a "popular" style, lots of strings) and also that it is helping the detective to get to "know" Laura.

Pursuing information about Laura, the detective goes to a restaurant with Waldo Lydecker (Clifton Webb). As the camera enters the restaurant, three musicians are seen, preparing to play. As the camera passes them, the musicians begin to play the same theme. Now it is doubly clear that this music is popular in this film world. But its association with Laura in the detective's mind is stressed, as fragments of it are heard in solo violin, slowed down and with tight vibrato and almost whining tone, somehow going with nostalgia expressed by Waldo. Each time these are heard, the quality of this "Laura" can almost be *seen* to be impressed into the psyche of the listening detective, as the camera returns to the table from flashbacks into Waldo's anecdotes about this very attractive creature. Now the way is paved for two extensions of the music—one private and into the interior of the detective's psyche and heard as a quality of someone special and lovely, the other back into the public world of the characters after Laura has returned, played by a typical 1940s dance band— all brass, winds, and percussion. These extensions seem to be effected largely by variation in instrumentation and pace.

In the public extension of the music, rather than appearing as someone special, Laura is seen as a member of a large gathering, several of whom (in the detective's mind), including Laura, might have committed murder. The private extension appears in a scene earlier where the detective is alone in Laura's apartment prior to her return, drinking her scotch, looking up at her portrait, musing and seemingly collecting into one impression all that he has learned of her and simultaneously felt. The theme becomes a love song. Here it appears highlighted by muted trombone and again briefly by piano. Although to many people muted brass may not ordinarily be associated with love songs, the muted trombone has here a peculiar hollow, spatial quality seemingly consonant with the loneliness and need of a lover. Piano rendition at this point may also connect with audience reminiscences of Romantic music of the nineteenth century, composed in large part for piano (by Chopin, exclusively for it).

But then the tones of this brief rendition begin to waver, at first as though the strings of the instrument may have been tampered with, or as though the piano is slightly out of tune. This wavering effect is quickly increased by a technical device to the point where the tones are no longer recognizable as those of a piano. These tones seem to be an auditory correlate of wavering lines of a mirage, indicating that the detective is trafficking here with something unreal, also complementing unclarity of his mental image of Laura, and/or a state of drunkenness. All of this is clearly a private affair with the detective. The music discloses the emotional condition of the detective to the audience, which the audience itself may or may not feel.

Finally, however, the musical score not only has a private and public aspect within this film world. It has also a private and public aspect to the audience. Unlike the detective, the individual moviegoer is not falling in love with this fictitious character (though the male moviegoer may be falling in love with the image of Gene Tierney and the female one with that of Dana Andrews). Yet the *Laura* theme is heard as hauntingly attractive and as suitable to the particular story, and also as translatable into the real "popular" world.

In a 1938 Russian film of Maxim Gorky's autobiographical trilogy, a great deal of music is made by the characters in the first part, entitled *Childhood*. The primary significance of this music seems to be the same to the characters as it is to the audience. Yet even in this case there are differences. A young gypsy man (variously addressed as Vanka, Vania, and Ivanka) who has been adopted by Alexei's grandparents, sings a song early in the film that becomes a theme song for Alexei and his friends when they are out in the fields. He sings this song when he is in the fields with Alexei also, and at one point says that if he had a good voice he would "go out into the world" and make his fortune. The song is thus associated with the freedom of the fields—as contrasted with the social life of the town—both by the characters in the film and by the audience. At the end of the film, however, as Alexei leaves his friends in the fields to "go out into the world" himself, he turns to wave goodbye to them, and the voice of the gypsy, who has been killed, is heard through the image of the boy. The song is heard through an orchestra and a "heavenly choir" as the boy is seen walking into the distant countryside. Finally, the song gains a significance to the audience beyond what it had to the characters. The friends in the fields surely hear no orchestra, no heavenly choir, nor presumably do they hear the gypsy's voice as they look at their friend waving goodbye. In this particular case, it seems that the ending detracts considerably from the unifying force of the song in the main body of the film. Whereas throughout the film, until the end, the audience has been at one with the characters, has been immersed in the story, the final treatment of the gypsy's song forces a more detached audience view for which there has been little preparation.

Both unity and connections of fiction with the real world have consistently functioned as criteria of evaluation of any art in any genre. However, this has not always been the case. I may not evaluate a work of art simply by noting that it is unified, in whatever sense "unified" is taken. Nor may I do this in noting that a fictional work is "realistic." Again, expression vocabulary appears to be valuationally contingent. I may praise a work in noting its expressive qualities, or remain valuationally neutral about it, or downgrade it, as in the following comment on *Winds of War* (1983): "The music [for *Winds of War*], including a nice original composition, has its overwrought flourishes. . . . See Hitler. Hear the loud, crashing music. See Franklin Roosevelt. Hear the soft, stirring music. Feel assured, proud."[12] We have noted in chapter one, however, that depth metaphor in music criticism, wherever it appears, is always valuational to the maximum positive degree. (Arnheim's understanding of depth in art also reflects this.) For all the significant functions that music may have in twentieth century cinema, we have yet to find here adequate explanation of this difference between descriptive and valuational terminology.

It may be the case that the best of film music cannot fairly be termed out-and-out shallow, in spite of the probable domination of immediate visual images that our analysis relates to shallowness. The partaking by film music of visual/literary depth, however, does not thereby appear to increase its independent musical depth. Indeed, music is typically viewed in cinema as an art of secondary importance. When in rare moments it rises to the fore and casts its own spell, we find ourselves looking elsewhere or shutting our eyes to the images on the screen. In general it appears that music not itself judged to be deep comes closest to effecting a quality of depth in film in its unifying functions or its transfer to the real world via double-entendre. But, as in film music's more limited functions, these still remain attached to what has primacy in vision and story.

NOTES

1. Rudolf Arnheim, *Picasso's Guernica: The Genesis of a Painting* (Berkeley and Los Angeles: University of California Press, 1962), 6.
2. Quoted by Tony Thomas, *Music for the Movies* (New York, London: Barnes-Tantivy, 1973), 164-165.
3. From a letter to the author by David Raksin. Continuing: "Vorkapich's solutions are better in some places than in others. But only a fool would think less than thrice about second guessing a man of that rank." This film was not released through regular channels.
4. *Music for the Movies*, op. cit., 117.
5. Jack J. Jorgens, *Shakespeare on Film* (Bloomington, Ill., and London: Indiana University Press, 1977), 217.
6. Ibid.
7. Hubert Clifford, quoted in Roger Manvell and John Huntley, *The Technique of Film Music* (London and New York: Focal Press, 1957), 79.
8. Ibid., 93.
9. *Music for the Movies*, op. cit., 116, 84.
10. Ibid., 117.

11. "Richard III: The Preservation of a Film," *Quarterly of Film, Radio, and Television* 11 (1957):280-293.

12. *The Tribune* (Oakland, Calif., February 4, 1983, sec., C-5).

Four

Fundamental Matters

I

In the space-time world, we distinguish the objective from the subjective, the public from the private. These distinctions presuppose the drawing of numerical identities. What is subjective and private is "personal." Persons have bodies that are numerically distinct from one another, and what is objective and public is numerically *other* from a person. As well as having bodies, however, persons also have feelings and harbor attitudes that cannot be heard, seen, or touched. Feelings may have only qualitative identity, but it is when feelings are regarded as having spatial location *inside* seen or touched animate bodies that problems about their relation to things numerically differentiated seem to arise. This appears to be the primary basis from which "expression" theories of art derive and the primary source of difficulties that these theories encounter. Technical distinctions that may be or have been drawn between expression and representation, or between expression and symbolization, need not be entered into here. It is enough that sources of at least some problems of these and other primarily valuational distinctions be traced.

As we have seen in the case of synchronized motion picture soundtracks, auditory perceptions may be related to visual perceptions in a fixed, determinate way. In the real world, however, this is ordinarily not the case. Connections between what is heard and what is seen or touched seem ordinarily to be ambiguous. We can interpret whining noises, for example, related to a box at which we are no longer looking, as indicating that the box is moving rapidly toward or away from us. Or, alternatively, we can attribute the whining noises as properties of a stationary box, i.e., we can think of the box as having among its properties that it makes certain whining noises.[1] The average American who has not been in jungles may learn about the properties of jungles through the movies. Thus, the sound of cockatoos or myna birds may conjure up for him an image of a staggering "drunk" British actor, glass in hand, saying: "Another night in this rain-soaked jungle and I'll go out of my mind!" In such fashion, the bird sounds become properties of a stationary—though vaguely located—jungle. Or the *timbre* of a bassoon may become a property of a fat man, that of an accordion a property of a French café or an Italian street vendor. Independently of conditioning through motion pictures, certain natural connections may be found, for example, between sounds of crashing objects and cymbals, of waterfalls and glissando harp, of a hoarse human voice and *timbre* of a saxophone.

It appears generally easier to hear sounds or music as properties of stationary objects seen or touched in space, than of activities or events also occurring through time. Invariance of musical connections in the latter cases appears more difficult to establish, in spite of the fact that music in movies, where such connections are generally established, carries through the temporal dimension. The theme of the characteristic American cinema score carries through all kinds of visual events. When it pervades an entire film, its function more often is to unify (in the sense of the last chapter) all events, or to act as a commentary of an unseen speaker about "the whole sorry mess."

Questions of artistic expression have in large part been questions about feelings and emotions not observable in the spatial world by vision, touch, or hearing. It has been suggested that language about feelings and emotions related to visual art does not connect with questions about spatial location. Hence theories of empathy or of projection intended to explain how feeling qualities come to be predicated of inanimate objects are seen as based on a misunderstanding of how we play a feeling language game.[2] This is all properly Wittgensteinian, but it leaves us without explanation of a feeling language game apparently operating independently of numerical identification. In the light of fundamental semiotic understanding of subject-predicate language forms, or even logicians' number references to events as *at* t_1, t_2, . . . t_n, it is difficult to see how the drawing of qualitative identities in specific descriptions of artworks can operate without presupposition of numerical differentiation as well. Perhaps this should be easiest to do in the case of auditory art, where music has no spatial location. The problem persists, however, when music is thought of as a "work" or a "composition"—as identifiable by opus number, and a logical constant. We are thus led to a view of the musical work as analogous to a visual, and most likely stationary, spatial model. The musical work exists separated from the person who hears it, and it is now thought of as having "properties." These properties appear to be of only two kinds: they are either literal or expressive. Within this *exclusive* literal-expressive framework of numerical constants, the quality of "depth" in music as we have analyzed it is nowhere.

In the light of the transiency and imprecision of auditory perception, one would expect demonstration of constancy of properties that are known through "external" senses to be made through visual, rather than auditory perception. This is just how Nelson Goodman proceeds, in identifying literal properties of musical works through the visually accessible marks of the notational musical score. Be it noted also that a score is a spatially located, stationary object whose *performances* are events at t_1, t_2, etc. "A score, whether or not ever used as a guide for performance, has as a primary function the authoritative identification of a work from performance to performance."[3] Goodman's analysis is sufficiently precise to allow his conclusion that "performances differing by just one note" are not instances of the same musical work.[4] It should be noted here that, where this conclusion has struck many as maddening and nit-picking, such criticism has been based primarily on auditory identification of a musical work, rather than upon Goodman's primarily visual identification. This is implied in the following criticism: "If, amid the morass of notes that constitute, for example, the climax of one of Tony Bruckner's little symphonic edifices, an inner, very inner note that can only be heard by the dog in the Airwatch helicopter is misplayed, is the piece a different work for the 3.1417 of the audience who may have heard it; what about the rest?"[5]

Tactual as well as visual criteria may also determine literal properties of a musical work. Marks in the musical notational system that Goodman has in mind—especially multiple staffs and multiple and necessarily different clef marks (treble and bass)—

presuppose a keyboard instrument as a performing condition even though no mark indicating this is on the score. Multiple staffs and clefs, as the student begins with in the study of elementary harmonic structure, not only tie notation to a spatially located keyboard instrument having greater pitch range than any other single performing medium, but also to a tactual, specifically a fingering determination of possible performance. Many passages of Domenico Scarlatti's keyboard sonatas could not have been performed without the introduction of the fingering possibility of the "turned thumb." An amusing excerpt from a letter describing the ineptitude of new members of a small-town, eighteenth-century orchestra indicates an intimate relation between notational conditions visually apprehended, and tactual possibilities:

> Bamboozler, our keyboardist, has fine hands. But he is unable to put them to good use except when the governess, hired by the mother, excuses herself for a moment, leaving him alone with his young lady students. The mechanics of fingering are completely unknown to him. In right-hand trills, he uses only the second and third fingers, refusing to allow the third and fourth to play on any account. In playing three part chords in the right hand in which the lowest tones lie a fourth apart and the upper a third (par ex. *d*, *g*, *b*) he uses the second, third, and fifth fingers, even though the middle tone must be played by the fourth. And so, from the beginning, he ruins his students' hands. Also, he is so bad at thorough-bass that he knows neither the tones nor the tonality of the chord of the augmented second. In accompanying he is like the lowliest chorale player; he leaps all over the keyboard from one octave to another with his right hand, as if the identity of chords were known to him only here and there. And another proof that he knows nothing about harmony: not only does he play all mistakes from poor copies of arias, he transcribes them note for note in his students' copy books.[6]

Thus it appears that the identification of literal properties of non-spatial musical works in a visually accessible score has carried with it, in scores having multiple staffs and clef marks, further spatial reference to a keyboard performing medium, together with a score structure that has been determined in part tactually.

What, then, are the conditions of "expressive" properties of a musical work? These are to be distinguished from literal properties in more than one way. First, they cannot be exclusively identified visually or visually/tactually. Expressive properties depend on hearing, and as such are more likely to be criticized as "subjective." Resulting from hearing, expressive properties have no spatial location, yet their identification is based on an analogy with a visual or visual/tactual spatial model that allows numerical differentiation between the person judging and the object judged. The assumption in the very distinction of expression has a "property" of an "object" or "work" is that expression has objectivity, that it can be identified along with literal properties as independent of a particular individual's judgment. The primary means of demonstrating this objectivity is through the determination of expressive properties as constants of numerically identified musical works. This, in turn, depends either upon drawing a logical difference between what an individual himself feels and what he finds in the object, or upon an empirical observation that, in fact, I may not myself feel the particular quality that I attribute to the work. Thus, even feeling qualities of the work and feelings I have myself maintain numerical as well as qualitative differentiation. It should be noted here that where the sole access to this difference is auditory, such difference appears most difficult to grasp and maintain.

Although the musical work is taken to be an object in the space-time world, it is not taken to be animate or sensate. It appears necessary to apply to it the notion of "intentional object" when we attribute to it expressed feelings, emotions, or attitudes. How might both literal and expressed properties thus thought of be found exemplified in a particular work? We might find that in standard practice of tonal composition, for example, the one-six-four chord functions well to introduce a development section. When the root of the six-four chord is not in bass position, we may note the chord's expressive property of "hanging" unsupported, like an unsupported object hanging in space. We might then also find that we could anthropomorphize or intentionalize this description and say that the one-six-four chord is used to "invite" thematic development. Such a description can be made of a particular work and of musical works within the system of tonal composition generally. Again, we might metaphorically relate the typical ending of a tonal composition on V-I to "firmly grounded" objects in space or (alternately) intentionally as ending "with conviction." (We may typically see the keyboard performer at this cadence bring his head emphatically downward, perhaps slightly bouncing it, as a head might do it if had literally hit bottom). Or we might draw an analogy with logic and say that the dominant at typical points in tonal composition "implies" the tonic, or, alternately, that it "anticipates" the tonic.[7] These may be taken to be examples of Goodman's understanding of expression as "metaphorical exemplification," where such exemplification has, within broad cultural limits, a constant relation to literal properties of musical works.

The assumed constancy of music's expressive properties has been evident in psychological experiments designed to determine whether there is indeed such a thing as musical expression. Within the conceptual scheme of literal and expressive properties, however, such psychological check has seemed to require experimental controls. Yet there has been virtually no agreement among investigators as to what these controls should be, nor any theoretical basis for establishing them. There has been disagreement over the use of adjective checklists, especially in instructions for responses given to subjects, and in standards for determining "right" and "wrong" responses. Further disagreements in use of controls have appeared over frequent presentation of detached musical tones, intervals, or chords to subjects, rather than complete phrases or whole compositions; over the use of phonograph recordings rather than live performances; over methods for determining the musicality and training of subjects, and over other accounts to be kept of them. Together with varying definitions of the terms *expression* and *emotion,* and references to the possible influence of unrecognized social factors upon data collected, the general picture of methodology in this area of psychological experimentation is extremely confused.[8] Indeed, Kate Hevner, whose results are still considered among the most reliable, found that "our social and cultural inheritance is so important and effective in building up our habits of perception and apprehension that it is impossible to conceive of experimental conditions which would control them. . . ."[9]

V. A. Howard has referred to Hevner's experimental results as significant verification of Nelson Goodman's "constancy thesis" that is, "that if music expresses, it does so by virtue of some . . . literal properties of music."[10] Howard, however, interprets Hevner's "mood" adjectives as referring to properties that particular music "metaphorically exemplifies," in other words, to qualities the music is heard to have, rather than to moods aroused in the listeners themselves. Yet Hevner clearly indicated that "by expressiveness . . . we mean the immediate and direct responses which the organism makes to [musical sounds], especially such psychological responses as motor attitudes, empathic experiences, affective states, mood effects and emotional reactions, since the sentiments or concepts or ideas which may also be aroused are largely conditioned by these psychological responses."[11] This is not to say that other psychologists have not drawn a distinction: Harvey L. Decker noted that "we want to avoid a common confusion regarding the meaning of the word 'expression.' The confusion here is one of reference, i.e., of whether the 'expression' of emotion by music refers to some emotion aroused *in the listener* by the music, or, instead, to a musical portrayal, depiction, representation or symbolization of an emotion recognized but not necessarily experienced by the listener."[12] This only indicates more clearly general inconsistencies among psychological investigations.

Besides being assumed to be constants—at least within broad cultural limits—expressed emotions have consistently been taken to be differentiated from one another and to be the same emotions that have been known in past non-musical circumstances. If a judge were to say that emotion that he finds "expressed" in a particular work is utterly indescribable, has no name, and is not identifiable as any emotion he has felt elsewhere, he will likely be said to be misusing the term *expressed*. He will not be taken to be referring to any emotion-constant, thus not to an objective property of $Opus_n$. And feelings whose names range from near synonyms to logical contraries, such as Gurney detailed by example, which seem to be mixed up in some indescribable blur, apparently cannot be expressed by $Opus_n$.

How, then, do feeling qualities become properties of inanimate or insensate musical sounds? To confirm that there *is* such a thing as musical expression in this sense is one thing, but we are still in need of explanation as to how this occurs. As in Goodman's location of literal properties of a musical work visually, once more we can find analyses of musical expression by analogy with visual perception. S. Davies, for example, suggests that there are sound "appearances" analogous to visual "appearances" of feeling conditions. Looking first at what we see, Davies notes that "the emotion-characteristics in a person's appearance are given solely in his behaviour, bearing, facial expression and so forth. And, as a person's felt-emotion need not be expressed, it can be privately experienced in a way in which the emotion-characteristics in appearances can never be." Davies then draws an analogy with "emotion-characteristics in appearances" known visually with hearing musical sounds as "like human behavior," as "displaying intentionality." This, he thinks, derives primarily from musical dynamics, from "hear[ing] movement between notes." From this base, Davies attempts to explain "aesthetic response" to music in the recognition by the listener of "emotion-characteristics" that he hears "appearing" or displayed in it.[13]

Roman Ingarden's phenomenological account of the musical work, however, does not regard musical "motion" as a "sounding element" of a musical work, analogous to visually perceived motion of physical objects. Rather, Ingarden finds musical motion to be a sometime-result of what is heard.[14] Other limits might be found in Davies's account of the origin of emotional expression, for example, that it does not explain well such expression as may be found in a single, long-held note of Pavarotti that stimulates his audience to wild applause. It is unclear how an "expressive" note displays or gives an appearance of human intentionality, other than simply that it is sung by a human being.

Recent attempts to explain the origin of auditory expression through analogy with visual perceptions do not mention the synchronized soundtrack of motion pictures. Yet the more we study synchronizations of *immediate* visual and auditory impressions, difficulties increase in identifying a relation between them as "expressive." What we see and what we hear simultaneously may simply go together, belong together, with no independent similarity between them establishable. For example, most of the *leitmotifs* of Max Steiner for *Gone With the Wind* were distinctly Viennese in style. Yet somehow, they fit very well the characters and places set in the American Civil War South. And, rather than expressing her, the *leitmotif* for Melanie, for example, belonged to her, seemed more nearly to be one of her literal properties. It is difficult to point to any quality of her musical theme which independently connects with her personality or looks. Perhaps we could say that Melanie is a maudlin character—this identified partly by what we see in her facial expressions—and that her Viennese *leitmotif* is also maudlin, but that is not sufficient. Most of the *leitmotifs* for different characters in this film could be called maudlin, but other characters were not maudlin as Melanie was. Yet they fit their *leitmotifs.* The situation is more nearly that the characters acquired musical dimensions than that the musical themes expressed them. Even in Melanie's death scene, where her *leitmotif* is heard in slow and breathy rendition picking up qualities of her dying speech, this treatment seems no more to express her death than do the visual images of Melanie lying supine in bed. Like her dying speech, it appears more nearly as auditory evidence of her death.

Whatever difficulties may be encountered in attempts to explain expressive qualities in music through analogies with visual perception, however, it seems likely that some such connection will have to be claimed if a solely auditory world would be, as Strawson and Ayer posited, a solipsistic one. Within a solipsistic world, it seems that no numerical identities having literal or expressive properties could be distinguished. Goodman has termed his understanding of a work of art "physicalistic," and has regarded it a "mistake" to "locate [phenonenalistically] the aesthetic in the immediate and uninterpreted."[15] Monroe Beardsley's account of "aesthetic objects" is compatible with Goodman's in these respects. What such physicalistic understanding fails to provide, however, is ground for explicating, among other qualities, depth or profundity in art. Our analysis of depth metaphor in music criticism, on the other hand, has not counted "locating" the aesthetic in the immediate and uninterpreted to *be* a mistake. The locating (tracing) of a major aesthetic quality of music—depth— in a theory of partial recall of prenatal experience cannot maintain a difference drawn by Goodman (and others) between a musical work and its performances. Musical sounds heard as analogous to a prenatal sound complex are not related to that complex as musical performances are related to works performed. The prenatal sound complex is disanalogous to a musical work in that it is not a human construct, not properly regarded as an intentional object, and a recorded playback is not of its *performance.* The playback is a reproduction of the same thing. Our explication of depth in music is based on a different epistemological and metaphysical scheme from that of the physicalist. If what is known (experienced? cognized?) is always taken to be dependent on *some* sense perception, then our case has been based solely on

auditory perception. But any metaphysical base our account has
draws no distinction between the objective and subjective, the
universal and particular, the public and private. Essentially, we
have regarded the Rastafarian, through his combined use of marijuana and reggae, as retreating to solipsism.

As we have seen, a physicalistic understanding of the work of
art entails a logical distinction between feeling or emotional qualities possessed by the work and feelings or emotions that the
judge of the work himself may experience. In music, the example
we are given *ad nauseum* is that to say "the music is sad" is not to
say that I, the judge, feel sad. Here again the physicalistic scheme
fails to explain the fact that the quality of depth—presumably a
property of a musical "work"—is *always* felt by the one who
finds it, and felt deeply. In actual usage, the term *deep* in a
valuational as well as a descriptive sense does not maintain this
distinction between a property of an "object" and a "subjective"
feeling. This appears to be the case not only in music criticism;
often philosophy itself is judged aesthetically in point of profundity. We are told that Wittgenstein's philosophy is profound,
but that Strawson's philosophy is shallow. Now, if there is a
logical contradiction on page twelve, say, we presume that the
contradiction will be there whether anybody finds it or not, in
quite an "objective" way. But if profundity is to be found on
page twelve, we, the judges, must *find* it and *feel* it. If profundity
is a property of Wittgenstein's philosophy, it is also a quality felt
(quite intensely) by the Wittgenstein scholar.

Susanne Langer's understanding of expression as symbolization does not clearly maintain a physicalistic objective-subjective
distinction, in spite of her otherwise "objective" account of art
works as having common distinguishable characteristics that other
things lack.[16] Beginning her development of Ernst Cassirer's
theory of symbolism with specific consideration of the art of
music, Langer finds that music "articulates forms of feeling" as a
"non-discursive" or "presentational symbol." She finds an iso-
morphic relation between dynamics of musical form and the
dynamic forms of human existence, the "vital, sentient forms of
being."[17] Serious questions have been raised about the possibility
of any symbol being "presentational"—what could this mean?[18]
But Langer's description of music as a "felt quality" that is "not
logically discriminated" or "recognized as a function,"[19] is at

variance with physicalistic accounts in a more extended way. In her failure to distinguish "felt quality" from what is heard, Langer has achieved a description of music beyond the constraints of physicalism and their logical consequences. Hanslick's presupposition was that if we cannot find primary significance in music via expression, then we must find it in musical form. In Langer's exposition, form and expression merge. Gurney's empirically based suggestion (as we have interpreted *The Power of Sound*) that there is another source of aesthetic value in music besides form or expression accommodates Langer's account better than does Hanslick's, but it avoids the logical problems inherent in Langer's distinction of a "presentational symbol." If we agree, however, that her account is not of a symbolic relation, we may still find a logical problem in that account in separating feeling qualities that music is heard to have from qualities felt by a judge. Many have found Langer's account challenging, but this may well have been independent of her theory of symbol. Indeed, it appears in such as the following quotation that what Langer achieved was a detailed description of the quality we have called depth in music, and that (however vaguely) she realized that this quality *could not* be explicated successfully within the disjunctively exclusive dichotomy of objectivity-subjectivity. Yet remaining (as she apparently wished to do) within the objective world, there was available to her no other model of explication than one based precisely on that disjunctive difference.

The assignment of meanings is a shifting, kaleidoscopic play, probably below the threshold of consciousness, certainly outside the pale of discursive thinking. The imagination that responds to music is personal and associative and logical, tinged with affect, tinged with bodily rhythm, tinged with dream, but *concerned* with a wealth of wordless knowledge, its whole knowledge of emotional and organic experience, of vital impulse, balance, conflict, the *ways* of living and dying and feeling. . . . Not communication but insight is the gift of music; in very naive phrase, a knowledge of "how feelings go." This has nothing to do with *"Affektenlehre,"* it is much more subtle, complex, protean, and much more important; for its entire record is emotional satisfaction, intellectual confidence, and *musical* understanding. "Thus music has fulfilled its mission whenever our hearts are satisfied."[20]

One suspects that Langer's insight was established independently of her support of Cassirer's theory of symbol, and that the seven chapters preceding chapter eight in *Philosophy in a New Key* did not really dictate what of "significance" she has found in the art of music. Where some have thought: "She *has* something there," we can still expect the physicalist to ask: "Puzzle: what's wrong with this picture?"

II

The physicalistic view of a work of art is open to the question of how we move from descriptions of properties of "objective" works to their aesthetic evaluation. Can we not reduce all evaluations to descriptions? One of the most extensive attempts to answer this difficult question has been made by Monroe Beardsley in *Aesthetics: Problems in the Philosophy of Criticism*. Among objective qualities of a work of art, Beardsley includes what he terms "human regional qualities." We presume that he would regard what we have termed "depth" to be one of these. These qualities figure prominently in his analysis of "critical evaluation" of art. Beardsley finds that these qualities are not *ipso facto* good or bad, and do not by their presence alone determine whether a work is praised or downgraded. Indeed, he argues against any aesthetic value being "intrinsic," and he favors an "instrumental" function of three primary "General Canons" in artistic evaluation: unity, complexity, and intensity of quality. Unity, complexity, and intensity of quality vary in degree. Although reference to one of them—unity, for instance—does not always mark a positive evaluation, it is likely that one or another of these three qualities, or some combination of them, or a lack of them, will determine a general judgment that a work is good or bad.[21]

Some of Beardsley's analysis depends upon inquiry into linguistic functions of valuational vocabulary. When a critic says that a painting is good, we are entitled to ask "why?" This, then, involves the critic in "critical reasoning" that may include considerable dispute and argumentation. Beardsley argues against theories that critical language is really a "performatory act" on the part of the critic (this "assimilates critical evaluations to nonlinguistic acts"), or that critical language is a disguised combination of exclamations and imperatives.[22] He argues vigorously against "relativism," where apparent critical contradictions are taken to be "not real contradictions." However variable particular judgments may be, Beardsley does not find that this entails variability of general critical judgment. "If more people like the poems of Anne Morrow Lindbergh than like the poems of Dylan Thomas or W. H. Auden, this does not mean that they would all say that they think her poems are better poems."[23] What is more important than variability of individual judgments, he finds, is variability of critical reasons, where disputes "move down into basic questions."[24]

An instrumental view of qualities deemed valuable requires an answer to the question: what are they valuable for? But rather than positing some final "intrinsic" value, Beardsley finds values in art to be instrumental in production of "aesthetic experience."

> The Instrumentalist definition of "aesthetic value," . . . is carefully framed to expose the fact that to adopt it is to take for granted that something is already known to be valuable, namely aesthetic experience. It makes the value of the aesthetic object a means to an end. But of course we are immediately confronted with a further question, about the value of the end itself: what justifies the assumption that this experience is valuable? . . . [However, the question of whether aesthetic experience is valuable] is not the question of whether it is enjoyable, but the question whether its enjoyment can be justified, in comparison with other enjoyments that are available to us as human beings, as citizens in a twentieth century democratic society. . . . You can never judge the value of anything except in relation to other things that are *at that time* taken to be valuable. . . . If an object were intrinsically valuable, no reason could be given to prove it . . . , since the reason would consist in pointing out its connections with other things, but if the value depends upon those connections, then it is not intrinsic. The value would have to be self-evident in some way. Yet if I start with the stove [for example] and trace its consequences and their consequences, I do not seem ever to get to anything that is self-evidently valuable.[25]

Beardsley's account of evaluation of art does not accommodate the quality of depth in music at all well. (1) Not just in music, but wherever it appears, the quality of depth or profundity does not vary in degree. Although works even in different genres can be comparatively evaluated on the basis of depth, such works are

either deep or they are not. Although it appears that depth *can* be thought of as among their objective properties, this quality is apparently also always "felt deeply" by the judge. (2) Some major critical judgments do not appear to entail the giving of reasons. A judgment, "Beethoven's *Coriolan* overture is deep," is not clearly open to the question "why?"; it does not seem to involve the judge in "critical reasoning." It is more nearly a report of something that, presumably, everyone hearing it will understand—as we have it analyzed, a report of recognition and recall (however unconscious) of a dynamic feeling *gestalt* (which Susanne Langer seems to be describing above) that all humans have known and therefore should be able to recognize. (3) Such human recognition is of something having positive intrinsic, not instrumental value.*
By our analysis of depth metaphor in music criticism, there is intrinsic maximum positive value in *being alive* under circumstances that have never been faced with adversity. This is found, so to speak, "in the living" and is self-evident. We do find intrinsic value in the *fact* of human life, and thus ideally wish to extend it forever. Thus, death is the maximum tragedy. For the most part, murder and suicide are regarded as evidence that the actor is sick or in some other way has lost his sense of this intrinsic

---

*I use here two criteria for identification of intrinsic value: (1) Intrinsic value is a value which is self-evident, for which no reason can be given. (2) It is a value found by everyone, and in that sense universal. (See Section III of this chapter for further extensions.) Apparently it is sometimes assumed that a third criterion is also necessary, i.e., that intrinsic value be indestructable or eternal. Presumably, such a value never could be found or tested empirically. However, indestructability seems to be more nearly a *result* of finding intrinsic value, rather than a condition of its identification. That is, we first find a value that is self-evident and universal (as in the fact of being alive under circumstances not faced with adversity) and then wish it to last forever. So, we pray for eternal life.
This identification of intrinsic value is contrary to Beardsley's own conclusion that intrinsic value cannot be identified. Beardsley's primary argument against "empirical" defense of intrinsic value by C. I. Lewis and others is that they confuse what is valued with what is valuable, what is desired or liked with what is desirable or likeable. And *justification* of what is valued by one individual Beardsley finds to be dependent on "a wider context of other things, in relation to a segment of a life or of many lives." ("Intrinsic Value," *Philosophy and Phenomenological Research* 26 [1965]: 13). Our second criterion that intrinsic value is a value found by all humans, however, appears to merge what is valued with what is valuable.

value—or else we justify his acts because they result from a *particular* life that is faced with adversity.* (4) No "General Canon" referred to by itself or in combination with other "canons" invariably functions in a positive evaluation. Depth, on the other hand, is always maximally positive in function wherever it appears. It thus fits uneasily among "human regional qualities." Beardsley's own metaphor of "region," again spatial, does not relate well to the spatial metaphor of depth.

Difficulties of physicalistic value theory appear greatest in cases where the qualities valued do not vary in degree and are not clearly or exclusively identifiable as properties of objects. Suppose I am asked what Mozart's music "has" that Salieri's does not? Suppose I give a typical answer that Salieri's music is commonplace, but that Mozart's music, again and again, is immediately grasped by all humans, has universal affective appeal. Now, universal human-outreach can hardly be considered a property or quality of Mozart's music. It is easier to think of "the commonplace" as a property of Salieri's music, but even this isn't exactly clear. One may further note that the "universal" and the "commonplace" have, so to speak, "something in common."

Yet how can I praise Mozart's music to the maximum for its universality and downgrade Salieri's for being commonplace? Only this seems to be the difference: What I find of universal human outreach "affects me profoundly"—am I not among all those humans reached? But what is commonplace "leaves me cold." Now clearly, my reasons do not refer to properties of any musical composition, but rather to my own and to other people's feelings. This is not to say that I cannot also evaluate Mozart's and Salieri's music objectively by reference to Beardsley's three criteria. But such basis of evaluation does not explain how something can be maximum good if it is "universal" and not good if it is "commonplace."

Claims that music is a universal language appear to connect with judgments of music as deep. In this instance, we may reasonably regard use of the term *language* to be metaphorical. Stress should be placed on a claim that music is literally understood by

---

*This suggests a very rudimentary relation of moral value with aesthetic value, a connection sought in general theories of value.

all humans. The likeness of language used metaphorically to literal language seems to lie in a mutual understanding among humans that music and language both seem to effect. There is also couched in claims that music is a universal language, a clear, highly positive evaluation. (In contrast, we find no consistent valuational function in observations about literal language.) Moreover, suggestions that such evaluations are disguised imperatives made by the judge, as in Kant's "I demand that all men shall find it so," appear to evade a *real claim* to having found a universal ground of human evaluation. Again, Beardsley's criteria, which would be located as qualities of an objective musical work, do not accommodate these circumstances. What we must do, to remain within the physicalistic scheme, is to argue that such extra-objective references can be reduced to or translated into language referring specifically to musical "objects," and not to feelings of a judge. Perhaps *universally understood* really refers to a clearly unified structure; or to a complexity that we, the judges, are used to looking for; or to some intensity of quality which we hear, or to some mix of these. Yet none of this explains the reference to universality, other than suggesting that we simply have here a sloppy use of vocabulary. In the physicalistic world, we remain in a world of instrumental values and of valuational contingencies.

When universality is extended temporally, we get the valuational criterion of "durability." Here again, we do not have reference to a property of a work of art. If I say that "So-and-So's" musical composition won't last, but that such-and-such a novel "will live through the ages," I am not pointing to a property of that novel, nor to a property of that musical composition.

In evaluation, questions of profundity, and both spatial and temporal "universality," appear to entail a break-down of the subject-object dichotomy. As Hegel put it in *The Philosophy of Fine Art*, the distinction "falls away." Within the physicalistic fence of both logical restrictions and artistic evaluations, we don't clearly know to what we refer when we use such vocabulary. Equally important to recognize is that art based specifically on auditory perception, not on visual/tactual perception, may take us out of the space-time world that presumably we begin to know at birth, and provide for us an avenue of retreat to a solipsistic or semi-solipsistic state that is both intrinsically valuable and literally universal. Sometimes this is termed *freedom*, sometimes also, *peace*. Often it connects with mysticism and religion. Philosophically it connects with metaphysical idealism. Of meta-physical idealists, however, only Schopenhauer and Nietzsche appear to have clearly recognized the special importance of music, and thus, by implication, something of the unique status of auditory perception in art which Edmund Gurney posited psycho-logically.

In a chapter titled "The Joint Revelation of Self and World," Albert Hofstadter acknowledges several "tendencies in modern thought, especially noticeable since Goethe and Kant, to bring opposites together into a synthetic unity. . . ." Concentrating on Jacques Maritain's *Creative Intuition in Art and Poetry*, Hofstadter finds that a "joint revelation theory has its own characteristic cluster of figures in terms of which it goes to work: self, thing, beyond, mystery, hidden meaning, convey, disclose, reveal, sign, password, divine, penetrate, pass through, grasp, spiritual com-munication. One needs only to collect such key pieces to awake immediately to the sense of the game that is being played with them."[26] Hofstadter gives details of this "game," which yet at-tempt to remain within a theory of sign or symbol:

> The work itself as a sign is dual; it reveals, manifests and discloses not only the inner side of things, but also the inner depth of the self. In this dual signifying, the self arrives at spiritual communica-tion with being; the mystery on this side joins with the mystery on that side to come forth, obscurely, still hiding much of itself, in the disclosure. Spiritual communication between the two is possi-ble because they are connatural: reality and subjectivity are like in nature or essence. Hence, since only like can know like, the self, through the emotion which imbues it, comes into an intentional (not mystical, magical, ontical) union with its opposite, reality or being or the infinite depth of things. . . . The poem—the musical composition, the painting, the work of art of whatever sort—is a made object that comes about in the creative objectification of the poetic intuition in which this knowledge through *affective union* [italics added] takes place. As the mind of the poet arrives at its affective union with objective reality, in which it discovers jointly a pre-existing depth of things and its own pre-existing (un-conscious) depth of self, it utters forth this knowledge in the words of the poem. Or, since the words of the poem are a unity, and the poem is a dual sign having the above-described unitary sense, we may say without distortion of the intent of Maritain's

theory that the poet's *word* emerges as the expression of this single knowing of the joint communication of the antecedently existing depth of the self and the world of things.[27]

Such use of language should cause a logician to throw up his hands. But Hofstadter criticizes Maritain's "joint revelation theory" on other grounds. It cannot, he finds, account for "genuine creativeness" in production of art.

All the work that creation normally performs [would have] been done already. . . . Is there not . . . reason to suppose that the "depths of meaning" of world and self are products of an activity that goes on in man and that constitutes his primary vision of the being of the world and self? If we speak of a meaning existing beforehand and ready to be disclosed, is this anything more than a reading back into the preliminary stage of what eventuates from that stage, a reading of actuality *backward* into possibility . . . ? The image of the work of art as revealing hidden content, thus, is unsatisfactory because it is inadequate to the actual experience of artistic creation. It is not unsatisfactory because it attributes to art the function of opening up to the human vision meaningful depths of the self and the world. It is unsatisfactory because it takes for granted the result of the creative struggle without having any ground for doing so; it removes from the creative struggle its creativity. If it could tell us beforehand what the creative struggle would achieve, we could then have sufficient reason to give the revelation theory our allegiance. But it is no wiser than any prophet after the event. It, too, has to wait until the artist has arrived at his intuition before it can tell us what the depths of meaning are that the artist has conquered.[28]

Hofstadter does not see logical difficulty of the kind Susanne Langer encountered in positing an expressive or symbolic function that obliterates the subject-object dichotomy. He apparently does not consider that Maritain's understanding of depth of self and world logically *could* not be something expressed or symbolized. But his observation that such "affective union" cannot be created by an artist appears correct, as does his recognition that if Maritain's account is correct, the artist must needs "read actuality backward into possibility." Hofstadter, however, does not recognize that this "backward reading" would have to involve some kind of memory, and does not then raise the further question of whether such memory is sensory in nature—for example, specifically auditory or visual. Writers who speak of depth and use the reference valuationally seem to typically assume that everyone will understand what is being referred to, that it is therefore not in need of explication, and do not even clearly recognize that the term is used metaphorically.

It does seem consistently to be assumed, however, that depth or "affective union" is not a product of logical deduction by some philosopher in the working out of a metaphysical or epistemological system (for example, Kant's "transcendental unity of apperception"), but is something known psychologically and empirically, involving both mind and sense perception, something universal, found in temporal retrogression of some kind, and something that—once pointed to—everyone will or should recognize. Hence, we find such close corollary terms as Hofstadter points out: mystery, hidden, beyond, reveal, penetrate, pass through, spiritual communication, almost all of which are spatial metaphors. Finally, although Hofstadter correctly implies that the finding of depth by the artist in Maritain's view is an essentially passive function of retrogression and is not "created" by an artist, he does not treat this as an invitation seriously to rethink the concept of artistic production of what is most highly prized as primarily creative—to ask whether or to what extent meritorious artistic production *is* creative. Creative production of what is new or original must be understood within a world of numerical identities and subject-object dichotomies, not within a state in which the observing self and what it senses are indistinguishable.

III

If there has been a problem in physicalist aesthetics of relating objective accounts of art to their evaluation, there has also been a problem for metaphysical idealists—in their "transcendental flights"—of maintaining contact with the obvious rooting of art in sense perception. If, on occasion, the subject-object dichotomy has seemed to fall away and the observer finds that he is communing with an aesthetic object in affective union, this has generally not been taken as a definitive situation for aesthetic theory. In his general theory of knowledge and valuation, C. I. Lewis has observed:

There is no need to erect a metaphysical mystery upon the fact that human purposes are marked by a considerable degree of community, enabling us on occasion to pass beyond actualities achieved to the esthetic purpose of them, and—in the case of music and the drama—to recreate from symbols the actualities which will approximate to and convey such intentions. These facts provide no better ground for being transcendentalist about esthetic goals than there is, for example, about economic ones or those of engineering; nor any better reason to invent an empyrean habitat for the esthetically ideal than there is to believe in some New Atlantis as a metaphysical reality.[29]

In *An Analysis of Knowledge and Valuation,* Lewis found common ground between empirical knowledge and the "immediately valuable." He hoped to frame a general theory of knowledge and valuation that would encompass more specific analyses in aesthetics as well as in ethics. "Evaluations," he noted, "are a form of empirical knowledge, not fundamentally different in what determines their truth or falsity, and what determines their validity or justification, from other kinds of empirical knowledge."[30] He, too, was concerned with the problem of relativism of empirical judgment, both in knowing and valuing; he, too, drew a distinction between intrinsic and what he termed extrinsic or objective value. Lewis did not deny the existence of intrinsic value, but he found it in immediate sense perceptions that do not constitute the making of value judgments. Empirical judgments are always subject to future verification. They may possibly be false. Thus, it is extrinsic values that are involved in value judgments that are a form of empirical knowledge. Objective value judgments are, in Lewis's terminology, "nonterminating." In this regard, they are the same as verifiable empirical judgments whose truth or falsity is always confirmable by future contingencies. "What I now believe has consequences which will be determinable indefinitely in the future."[31] On the other hand, immediate "presentations" of sense perception that are found to be "good" or that afford "satisfaction" and that have "intrinsic" value, are as they are to the individual who finds them. They cannot be false and do not constitute knowledge judgments. This is not to say that they cannot be formulated in a "report" of what is found.[32] It is "direct experienced goodness or badness, like seen redness or felt hardness [that ultimately] . . . give meaning to nonterminating value judgments. . . . Without the experience of felt value and disvalue, evaluations in general would have no meaning. . . . Objective value is at bottom derivative from direct appreciation; beauty is not finally determinable apart from the delight of some beholder; and nothing is good except relative to some possible felt goodness."[33]

Maintaining the subject-object distinction of traditional empiricism, Lewis distinguished intrinsic value from inherent value found in esthetic objects. Judgments of inherent value in aesthetic objects are extrinsic and objective, and thus predict "further value findings" indefinitely into the future. "The conception of [an aesthetic object] as a potentiality for conducing to certain positive value-qualities in experience, represents esthetic or inherent value in an object as an independent property of it, one which, like other properties, is tested by experience, but is not relative to any particular experience or to the value findings of the individual."[34] Aesthetic objects must possess inherent value in reliable form, Lewis found, and are only secondarily instrumental to other goods. They should be of a high order, providing justification for valuational predictions.

In his review of Lewis's book, W. T. Stace raised a primary question:

> Any theory of value which is 'subjective' in the sense that it holds basic value findings to be simply likings and dislikings, but yet wishes to avoid the extreme relativism which is now fashionable and to find value judgments objective and normative must necessarily introduce the notion of a common human nature. It will have to maintain that there is a common structure of human personality, compatible with wide differences in inessentials, just as there is a common structure of the human body . . . compatible with differences in colour of skin . . . and the like. It will try to show that upon this common structure of personality can be founded normative and universally valid value judgments. . . . Plato's tripartite soul is an early attempt of this kind. All that we find in Professor Lewis's philosophy, faintly suggesting a conception of this kind, are a few scattered passing references to the "solid core of what is both veridical and common, underlying the personal and interpersonal variabilities" and to "those capacities of apprehension which are common to humans in general." But this is not enough. The whole theory has to be worked out in detail. It seems to me that Professor Lewis has not realized that

without this a theory of value which aims to be normative and of universal human validity while yet finding immediate values in human likes and dislikes simply will not work.[35]

Some of the origin of the central problem that Stace finds may now be detailed. In his consideration of conditions of empirical knowledge, Lewis observed that memory must function in interpretation of immediate sense perceptions, and that "the common omission of this topic from epistemological studies is a bit of a scandal."[36] Although questions may be raised about the reliability of memory—perhaps one remembers incorrectly—"no empirical judgment can be validated solely by reference to immediately given facts of sense. It is also necessary, in order to justify any empirical judgment—even the terminating one 'If A then (probably) E'—that some generalization of the sort derived from past experience should be afforded."[37]

Although Lewis identified extrinsic value judgments as empirically verifiable statements having predictive value, he limited their origin to "immediate presentations" of intrinsic value. In this way, his theory cannot explain aesthetic value to be found in memory itself—a value with which some literary authors, notably Marcel Proust, have been centrally concerned. Nor can it find good ground for references to depth that clearly reach backward from immediate and individual "satisfactions" and "likings." Although Proust brought the past into the present in some sense, what he found was still not identical with present events, and its aesthetic value did not depend upon its being so. In Lewis's observation, "the past is irrecoverable: . . . [in the sense that] the presently given memorial items are not epistemically equivalent to the past experience which they represent, but are only surrogates of such past fact."[38] Still, Lewis's analysis could not regard them as having aesthetic value distinguishable from present sense perceptions.

Lewis did acknowledge a possible aesthetic role of memory, but an unimportant one, and one that did not identify aesthetic value of memory as rooted in a different function from that of memory in cognition:

There can be a diffuse and general value-aspect of experience which belongs to the background rather than to any item which stands out in it; one which the psychologist would attribute to the complexus of undiscriminated somatic sensations. Presentations are preponderantly mediations of the external senses, or memory or imagination, or else organic sensations which are specific and discriminated. But there is likely to be some vague remainder of the felt, not definitely localizable either in or out of the body. The sense-quality of this incohate remainder of given experience is relatively unformulatable even to ourselves, and the only clearly recognizable aspect of it is likely to be its value-character. When such background feeling rises to the level of attention, it most frequently does not attach to any presentation, but remains simply a general value-level of the experience as a whole. . . . [And] we but report a native fact of experience as it presents itself.[39]

One might well posit these comments as Lewis's response to our entire polemic, yet his and others' failure to differentiate between or to accomodate functions of memory in gaining empirical knowledge and functions of memory as aesthetically valuable appears itself to be a "bit of a scandal." Lewis regarded memory of the recent past as generally more epistemically reliable than memory of the more distant past. Yet, in aesthetic value of memory, quite the reverse seems to be the case. What we have seen or heard most recently sates us; we become victims of "sensory fatigue." And it was memory of the long-forgotten that carried with it for Proust the "all-powerful joy." There is more to observe, however, than that the long-forgotten may be free from sensory fatigue. It has not yet been suggested that if anything (in Stace's words) "common to human nature" is to be found, it is not to be found in reliable predictions of "nonterminating" aesthetic judgments, but may be found only in retrogressive investigations into whatever in sense perception may be, from birth or prior to birth, common to all human beings.

Yet more must be noted about the aesthetic in memory. Not only does it appear to relate to the distant and forgotten, rather than to the recent past; necessarily *by that fact* it relates to a time in early life when dangers to life were either nonexistent or almost so, and thus to a time in which living was marked by a near-continuous delight in everything sensed. We needed the wary and experienced older person to save us from being run over, from drowning, from falling into ditches, or drinking the poison on the bottom shelf. Our's was delight in that certain gorgeous shade of pink, or the new greenness of grass when we turned upside-down on the swing, or that certain turn in a melody that we waited for and savored, picking up the phonograph needle and dropping it down again on the "best" part, saving it as we saved the frosting on a piece of cake. We were not yet ready to say of our new "object" world: "It's a jungle out there!" We could not yet be expected to grasp the depth of tragedy, or possibly to understand the depths of Picasso's *Guernica*. For that, we would need to have lived in a world whose reality is dominated by vision, not hearing, and one in which the inevitability of death has been forced upon us. Until then, other people might die, but in our case surely there would be an exception.

This has sometimes been termed "childlike faith," and religions of the real world that promote it are understandably judged to be shallow in comprehension. But such comprehension would be dependent primarily upon visual or visual/tactual perception, upon language of subject-predicate distinction, upon logic, and Deweyan "experience" in the space-time world. It would fit the entire history of Western epistemology back to centuries B.C., but it would not fit early life of a dynamic, unfettered auditory *gestalt* of intrinsic value, nor Lewis's momentary "satisfactions" of this or that immediate "presentation." In addition, even if Lewis were right that value judgments *are* ultimately based on immediate perceptions, in judgments of depth or profundity that reference appears to be (in auditory perception at least) retrogressive rather than predictive. And Hofstadter was right: depth cannot be "created" by the artist; it is found by "going backward." Thus, when the critic finds it, as Lewis noted, he is making a "report" rather than engaging in (in Beardsley's terms) "critical reasoning."

We have traced the quality of depth specifically in auditory art to partial recall of a state in which dangers or contingencies in any human life did not exist, thus to a state having positive intrinsic and universal human value. It may have been assumed that such a state involves no sense perception at all, and thus should be considered as existing *prior* to the finding of "aesthetic values," but this is incorrect. Auditory perception is indelibly a part of it, and there is no good reason to think that an aesthetic state, in some viable sense of that excessively vague term, cannot be found in humans prior to birth.

As with other empirical and pragmatic philosophers—we have made special prior reference to Dewey—Lewis thought of psychology and epistemology in *blanket* perceptual terms. "Presentation to the senses" could be indiscriminately to any sense medium. Yet in illustrations, visual perception has predominated—indeed, ruled—in framing a world where subject and object are distinguishable. Stace may not have been clear in expecting that avoidance of relativism requires demonstration of a "common structure of human personality"—whatever *that* means. Still, at least constant function must be demonstrated in *some* sense perception; we have posited it to be in prenatal audition necessarily common to all human experience. This might be a positive step in satisfying Stace's expectation that Lewis's "whole theory needs to be worked out in detail." It now seems doubly clear that the secret to working out empirically any general aesthetic theory such as Beardsley's, or any general theory of value such as Lewis's, in detail that accommodates depth or profundity, lies in a recognition like Edmund Gurney's of a need to distinguish different sensory media as having different roles to play. And we may have here some explanation of what Lewis himself observed: "It is an obvious fact . . . that the science of esthetics remains largely undeveloped. . . . This indifferent success is doubtless attributable in part to the marked diversity which obtains amongst objects of aesthetic interest. . . ."[40]

Now, it may be argued that what we have termed an aesthetic quality of depth is not properly so identified, that no term that indiscriminately refers both to a property of an object and to the feeling of the judge is properly taken to refer to an "aesthetic value." It may be argued, in accordance with a distinction drawn by Beardsley,[41] that early sensory experiences should thus be thought of as having something more properly called *aesthetic power*, that they should be considered causes of aesthetic values and judgments, rather than values themselves.

This criticism obtains, it seems, only within a presupposed physicalistic understanding of aesthetic values as "inhering" in objects, and thus as waiting until a time when distinctions are clearly drawn between qualitative and numerical identities. In this way, a distinction between aesthetic power and aesthetic value begs the phenomenalist's question, and implicitly denies that anything properly called aesthetic value may be found in a solipsistic world. Yet we recall the smile of beatitude of the infant who hears once more that prenatal sound pattern, of the Rastafarian who is becalmed by marijuana and listening to reggae, or of a religious person or a mystic who, if only momentarily, wipes out the distinction between himself and what he "knows." There appears to be no good reason why their states cannot count as aesthetically valuable. Thus we seem finally to be left with a choice about depth-terminology in auditory art. Either we can argue that "depth" illegitimately appears in aesthetic value judgments in predicate place, or we can argue that actual usage warrants its appearance as predicate and that physicalistic or pragmatic theories such as those we have considered, in their primary dependence upon the subject-object distinction and in their orientation toward the future, are seriously limited both in aesthetic insight and in explanatory power. We have clearly taken the latter option.

IV

The first section of this chapter traces presuppositions that appear to be necessary in developing any theory of artistic expression, ultimately to drawing a distinction between qualitative and numerical identities. In the light of our explication of "depth" terminology in music criticism in chapter one, we have thus provided an explanation of why references to depth in music cannot be references to musical expression. We have further seen in sections two and three of this chapter that physicalistic or pragmatic theories of valuation do not offer good promise of explaining the consistently and maximally positive valuational function of depth metaphor in music criticism—a function that is implicitly non-relativistic. However, we have not yet considered the potentiality of phenomenological method (after Edmund Husserl) in accommodating our problems raised in chapter one. Perhaps there we did not need to dip into speculative psychology. Perhaps there are suggestions in phenomenology that may free us from hints of that Husserlian bugaboo, "psycologism."

Phenomenology has typically aimed at both detailed and comprehensive description of intuited "phenomena," without attempting an explanation of what is found in this "lived" experience. Noting that relations between consciousness and the world and between one consciousness and another are discontinuous and contingent, Maurice Merleau-Ponty objected to the fixed conceptualization and systematization imposed on the world by empirical science on the one hand and by logical and idealistic philosophy on the other.[42] From this orientation and also his concentration on sense perception, perhaps we can find better basis than those provided by theories considered in the previous sections for explaining an aesthetic vocabulary that at once refers to qualities of objects and to feelings of judges.

Merleau-Ponty, however, thought of different sense media as interdependent and as functioning in concert with the body. He did not recognize that auditory perception is established in humans well prior to either visual or significant tactual perception, and his understanding of sense perception connected with body animation does not allow for a prenatal condition in which bodily activity is radically restricted or non-existent. As with others, even with whom he otherwise disagreed, Merleau-Ponty's illustrations of sense perception were almost exclusively visual. As is implied in the title of his essay "Eye and Mind," it was vision related to body animation on which Merleau-Ponty concentrated. "Music," he noted, "is too far beyond the world and the designatable to depict anything but certain outlines of Being—its ebb and flow, its growth, its upheavals, its turbulence."[43]

In his writings on aesthetics, Merleau-Ponty did not seek a theory of the musical work independently of other artistic works (as did Roman Ingarden) such as his own brief references to music should have required. In sum, his understanding of sense perception suffered from the same perennial problem as have theories considered above: how to demonstrate or explain references to "ebb and flow," "growth," "upheavals," or "turbulence" of "Being" as always intrinsically and positively valuable. In accord with the phenomenological aim to describe but not to explain intuited phenomena, we might simply claim—as Merleau-Ponty seems to do in his aesthetic writing—that such positive aesthetic value is "just there," *found* as an invariant and essential element. But, of course, this is not always true. There is upheaval and turbulence in war and murder and in other things repugnant as well as good, and a musical work full of ebb and flow may be just awful. Merleau-Ponty's track of concentration on sense perception may have been essentially the right one. It remains apparent, however, that even accurate description of what is found "aesthetically" in auditory art cannot successfully be made unless consideration is given to different functions of different sense media. In *that*, it was Edmund Gurney who was on the right track.

Of phenomenologists who have been specifically concerned with "the arts," in inquiries about the musical work only Roman Ingarden seems to have recognized special need to concentrate solely on sound. In its early chapters, Ingarden's essay *The Work of Music and the Problem of Its Identity*, is an essentially negative account. The work "as such" is not any or all of its performances nor all of its possible performances. Much that is true of the work itself is not true of its performances, and vice-versa. Nor is the work identical with its score, or something "mental." If it is none of these, then, how can Ingarden's understanding of the nature of the musical work be based solely on sound? Ingarden regarded the work of music itself as a schematic reconstruction of processes of coming to know it, mainly through hearing sound-structures of its concrete performances. This "schema" is a "purely intentional object" and an "intersubjective" one. The work itself is not a sounding object, but derives from sound. It has no spatial or temporal existence, but, deriving from temporal events, it is "quasi-temporal." All of its parts or phases exist simultaneously, although they may be interdependent—a second phase, for example, dependent upon a first phase. But such phases do not follow one another in temporal order, any more than the number two comes in time after the number one. The musical work, then, is "supra-temporal." Since it exists in neither space nor in real time, it is not a "real object," but a purely intentional one. As a schematic reconstruction, the musical work is full of indeterminacies which are filled-in or "brought to concretion" in its individual performances.[44]

Like other phenomenologists, Ingarden generally objected to "subjective-objective" dichotomies in philosophy, and was an outspoken opponent of physicalism or what he termed "neopositivism." In a paper delivered at the Amsterdam University Institute of Aesthetics in March 1969, Ingarden looked historically at "subjectivity and objectivity" in aesthetics. "From time to time these two lines of inquiry met, but this usually meant that emphasis was placed upon one of them, that their differences were underlined. Thus, their separateness was maintained."[45] From his avoidance of the subjective-objective dichotomy alone, it is not surprising that Ingarden did not analyze the musical work as an "expression" of anything, and did not attempt to trace its "aesthetic values" to any of its formal characteristics. The musical work contains non-sounding as well as sounding elements, but expressions of, for example, emotions of sadness or terror are above and beyond the work. In characteristic phenomenological method, Ingarden concentrated on description. He did not attempt to explain the elements and moments he found characterizing the musical work, and inquiries into artistic and aesthetic values that he made elsewhere do not suggest sources of these values that might be different in auditory art from those in visual art or literature. Nevertheless, some of his observations about music fairly cry for pursuit of an explanation and in some cases come close to observations we have made on the grounding of value judgment specifically in auditory art. In chapter five, for example, Ingarden notes that what he terms *forms* or *structures* of the musical work typically recur over and over again, that this recurrence is peculiar to music and is "foreign to the structure of the literary work as such," that it seems to be an "essential agent" in European music, that it is intimately connected with emotional qualities and "affective" response, and that avoidance of this reiteration of basic forms in "modern music" also is accompanied by "striking diminution of emotional qualities." He also notes that in his opinion music, of all the arts, has the strongest immediate "affective" appeal. Yet we may note that strict recurrence in visual arts—such as in much ornamentation and decoration—produces boredom very quickly. We add to this Ingarden's own observation that this sort of recurrence is foreign to literary structure "as such," and the need of an explanation appears urgent: How does it happen that a repetitious structure that is foreign to literature, and that in visual arts typically produces boredom quickly, is the very one characterizing an art whose immediate affective appeal is strongest of all? Rather than faulting Ingarden for not attempting an explanation, however, one might give credit to phenomenological method as this particular philosopher developed it, in bringing out a need, in understanding the musical work, to concentrate solely on sound. Probably the Husserlian objection to "psychologism" would have prevented him from going the route of Edmund Gurney, or the eclectic route we have taken in chapter one. But the objection to the subjective-objective dichotomy such as physicalistic or neopositivist schemes require has in Ingarden's attempt to understand auditory art, yielded greater insight and brought him to the brink of the kind of psychological explanation we have attempted in this essay.

NOTES

1. See *Encyclopedia Britannica, Science and the Future*, Year Book (Chicago: Encyclopedia Britannica, Inc., 1982), 87.
2. B. R. Tilghman, *The Expression of Emotion in the Visual Arts: A Philosophical Inquiry* (The Hague: Martinus Nijhoff, 1970), ch.1.
3. Nelson Goodman, *Languages of Art* (Indianapolis and New York: Bobbs-Merrill, 1968), 128.
4. Ibid., 186.
5. From comments to the author by David Raksin, November 20, 1982.
6. Quoted by William J. Mitchell, Introduction to his English translation of C. P. E. Bach's *Essay on the True Art of Playing Keyboard Instruments* (New York: W. W. Norton & Co., Inc., 1949), 10.
7. This sort of demonstration has been made by Leonard B. Meyer in *Emotion and Meaning in Music* (Chicago: University of Chicago Press, 1961).
8. For questions on conditions of subjects' responses see: P. E. Vernon, "Method in Music Psychology," *American Journal of Psychology* 42 (1930):130-133; C. W. Valentine, "The Method of Comparison in Experiments with Musical Intervals and the Effect of Practice on the Appreciation of Discords," *British Journal of Psychology* 7 (1914-1915): 124; edited by Max Schoen *The Effects of Music*, 182, 140; Esther L. Gatewood, "A Study in the Use of Similes for Describing Music and its Effects," in *The Effects of Music*, 258; K. Brantley Watson, "The Nature and Measurement of Musical Meanings," *Psychological Monographs* 54, no. 2, (1942):4; Harvey L. Decker, "Experiments on the Musical Portrayal of Emotion," (Ph.D. dissertation, University of California, 1933), 139; Christian P. Heinlein, "The Affective Character of Major and Minor Modes of Music," *Journal of Comparative Psychology* 8 (1928):123.

For questions on "right" and "wrong" responses see: M. R. Trabue, "Scales for Measuring Judgment of Orchestral Music," *Journal of Educational Psychology* 14 (1923):556; Watson, op. cit., 7; Decker, op. cit., 14; M. J. Adler, "Music Appreciation: An Experimental Approach to its Measurement," *Archives of Psychology* 17, no. 110 (1929):10, 11, 78.

For questions on controlling musical stimuli see: C. S. Meyers and

C. W. Valentine, "A Study of the Individual Differences in Attitude Towards Tones," *British Journal of Psychology* (1914-1915):69; Kate Hevner, "The Affective Character of Major and Minor Modes in Music," *American Journal of Psychology* 47 (1935):105; Kate Hevner, "Experimental Studies of the Elements of Expression in Music," *American Journal of Psychology* 43 (1936):264.

For questions on manner of stimuli presentation see: Ralph H. Gundlach, "Factors Determining the Characterization of Musical Phrases," *American Journal of Psychology* 47 (1935):626; C. S. Myers, "Individual Differences in Listening to Music," *British Journal of Psychology* 13 (1922):52; C. E. Seashore, "Measure of Musical Talent: A Reply to Dr. Heinlein," *Psychological Review* 37 (1930): 182; Hevner, op. cit., 108; Vernon, op. cit., 133.

For questions on musicality and training of subjects see: David Bogen, "The Significance of Tonal Memory and Sense of Pitch in Musical Talent," *Psychological Bulletin* 30 (1933):599; E. G. Bugg, "An Experimental Study of Factors Influencing Consonance Judgments," *Psychological Monographs* 45, no. 201 (1933):23-47; J. P. Guilford and R. A. Hilton, "Some Configurational Properties of Short Musical Melodies," *Journal of Experimental Psychology* 16 (1933):35-53; Christian P. Heinlein, "Critique of the Seashore Consonance Test: A Reply to Dr. Larson," *Psychological Review* 36 (1929):524-539; J. A. Highsmith, "Selecting Musical Talent" *Musical Quarterly* 16 (1930):238, 242-245; James Mursell, "Measuring Musical Ability and Achievement: A Study of the Correlations of Seashore Test Scores and Other Variables," *Journal of Educational Research* 25 (1932):125; Schoen and Gatewood, op. cit., 137; June Downey, "A Musical Experiment," *American Journal of Psychology* 9 (1897):63; E. M. Edmonds and M. E. Smith, "The Phenomenological Description of Musical Intervals," *American Journal of Psychology* 34 (1923):278; Paul Farnsworth, "Ending Preferences Among the Three Positions of the Tonic Chord," *Journal of Comparative Psychology* 6 (1926):98; Gundlach, op. cit., 626; Myers and Valentine, op. cit., 120-121.

For questions on definition of terms see: W. Van Dyke Bingham, "Studies in Melody," *Psychological Monographs* 12, no.3 (1910):2-3; Decker, op. cit., 9-10; Hevner, "Expression in Music: A Discussion of Experimental Studies and Theories," *Psychological Review* 42 (1935): 186; Benjamin I. Gilman, "Report on an Experimental Test of Musical Expressiveness," *American Journal of Psychology* 5 (1892):42; C. C. Pratt, *The Meaning of Music* (New York and London: McGraw-Hill, 1931), 164 165, 177.

9. Kate Hevner, "The Affective Character of Major and Minor Modes," op. cit., 192-193.

10. "Music and Constant Comment," *Erkentniss* 12 (1978):80.

11. Kate Hevner, "Expression in Music: A Discussion of Experimental Studies and Theories," op. cit.

12. Harvey L. Decker, "Experiments on the Musical Portrayal of Emotion," op. cit., 9-10.

13. S. Davies, "The Expression of Emotion in Music," *Mind* 89, no. 353 (January 1980):67-86.

14. "The Work of Music and the Problem of Its Identity," in *Studia z estetyki* [*Studies in Aesthetics*], vol. II, ch. 5. Translated by Adam Czerniawski, edited by Jean G. Harrell, (Berkeley, Calif.: University of California Press, 1986).

15. "Some Notes on Languages of Art," *Journal of Philosophy* 47 (August 1970):566.

16. See Beardsley, *Aesthetics: Problems in the Philosophy of Criticism*, op. cit., 74.

17. *Philosophy in a New Key*, op. cit., ch. 8.

18. See especially, review of *Philosophy in a New Key* by Ernest Nagel, *Journal of Philosophy* 40 (1943):323-329. See also Beardsley, op. cit., 361.

19. See also, *Feeling and Form* (New York: Charles Scribner's Sons, 1953), 32.

20. *Philosophy in a New Key*, op. cit., 244.

21. Beardsley, *Aesthetics: Problems in the Philosophy of Criticism*, op. cit., ch. 11.

22. Ibid., ch. 10.

23. Ibid., 484.

24. Ibid., 485.

25. Ibid., 539, 541, 542.

26. Albert Hofstadter, *Truth and Art* (New York and London: Columbia University Press, 1962), 26, 27.

27. Ibid., 30, 32.

28. Ibid., 33-36.

29. C. I. Lewis, *An Analysis of Knowledge and Valuation* (LaSalle, Ill.: Open Court, 1950), 472.

30. Ibid., 364.

31. Ibid., 176.

32. By Lewis's analysis, the description of Joe Higgs in chapter one would be of this sort.

33. Lewis, *An Analysis of Knowledge and Valuation*, 384-385.

34. Ibid., 458-459.

35. "C. I. Lewis: *Analysis of Knowledge and Valuation*" *Mind* 57 (1948):85.

36. Lewis, op. cit., 333.

37. Ibid., 327.

38. Ibid., 354.

39. Ibid., 424-425.

40. Ibid., 469.

41. Beardsley, op. cit., 533.

42. See *Phenomenology of Perception,* translated by Colin Smith, (London: Routledge & Kegan Paul; New York: The Humanities Press, 1962).

43. Translated by Carlton Dallery in *The Primacy of Perception,* edited by James M. Edie, (Evanston, Ill.: Northwestern University Press, 1964), 161.

44. Of the few American authors who have been concerned with Ingarden's question of the nature of the musical work, Kingsley Price seems to have come closest to Ingarden's solution. See "What Is a Piece of Music?," *British Journal of Aesthetics* 22, no. 4, (Autumn 1982):322-336.

45. "Phenomenological Aesthetics: An Attempt at Defining Its Range," translated by Adam Czerniawski, *Journal of Aesthetics and Art Criticism* 33, no. 3, (1975):257.

Five

The Concept of Musical Genius

The spell [of Bethoven] is compounded of our feel-
ing that we will never understand his music to the
full, will never plumb its depths—and yet that we
do understand it very well.

George R. Marek
Beethoven: Biography of a Genius

The elements of musical works that Ingarden has detailed reflect that spectacular development in Western European music, almost all of it written by keyboard players, within approximately two hundred fifty years, and within approximately the same geographical location. The Polish scholar, Zofia Lissa, has criticized Ingarden's theory of the musical work as "historically limited. . . . Ingarden's ideas on music, its essence and features, are based on the responses evoked by the music he was acquainted with. The examples he mentions cover the range of composers from J. S. Bach to the early Strawiński. Their peculiarity was decisive for the formulation of Ingarden's views, although one cannot deny that his opinions are also valid for a wider range of musical works. Nonetheless, they are not universally valid. If we accepted the universal validity of Ingarden's ideas we should have to banish from the realm of music a great many phenomena that, from the perspective of the twentieth century, have been assumed as undoubtedly musical."[1] Ingarden's account, Lissa notes, does not consider electronic music. In a brief reply, however, Ingarden observed that when he wrote his work, electronic music was unknown, that his task as a phenomenologist was to analyze the empirically given without legislating *a priori* for every kind of music, including music as yet undiscovered.[2] We might add that it was the very spectacular nature of western European music that Ingarden's theory *did* address, its strong aesthetic appeal, that has been (perhaps in the history of all of music) the most in need of explanation and of well worked-out philosophical schemes to back it up. "For the first time," as one critic put it, "the halls were built for the music alone, not music made to fill the hall."[3]

Where he attempted explanation, Ingarden was not tempted to put his burden upon particular capacity or imagination of individual composers.

> In the circles of aestheticians of music, there is often talk of the "structuring" of tonal complexes. But such talk supposes that this structuring constitutes something—precisely the "structure"—which is imagined by the subject without any *fundamentum in re*. In my opinion, however, the structure is either sufficiently found-ed on the elements of a qualitative harmony or else finds in it a necessary but not sufficient condition, which must then be aug-mented by the subjective behavior of the aesthetically experi-encing subject; but it is only augmented and not freely created by the subject.[4]

It is clear that Ingarden found reiteration of certain musical "form" to be a primary *fundamentum in re*, at least in western European music.

We can again find recognition of importance of reiteration couched in the challenging work of German theoretician, Heinrich Schenker. Rather than being of a general form as with Ingarden, however, the reiteration on which Schenker's theory was based was a reiteration of certain tones—specifically, the tones of the tonic triad. Recognizing a "natural" connection between tones in the overtone series of any ground tone, Schenker interpreted western European composition of "the masters" as an "unfolding" (*Auskomponierung*, appearing on the score horizontally) of pri-mary tones of a triad, these tones consisting of a given ground tone and two other tones related to it as dominant and mediant. Much of the challenge of Schenker's theory lay in its implied explanation of the *quality* of the music that it purported to analyze. Heavily dependent upon recognition of "motion" throughout often long and complex compositions, we find subsidiary references of Schenker, for example, to "liveliness and activity of tones," "powerful development," "stronger and richer" development, "the form of the whole," "organic unity," and in Beethoven, the "effect of a closed conceptual unit."[5] Schenker clearly did not wish, any more than did Ingarden, to explain the spectacular qualities of Western European music by reference to the genius of particular individuals. "The feature of Nature [meaning the basic triadic *Ursatz* of a tonal composition] cannot be rejected by *any* [italics added] genius but can at most be replaced at certain times by modifying surrogates. . . ."[6] Schenker's analysis interpreted successful tonal composition to be established on a "rational common foundation."[7] Schenker's understanding of musical genius was as a function clearly guided by natural principles. "A great talent or a man of genius, like a sleepwalker, often finds the right way, even when his instinct is thwarted by one thing or another. . . . The superior force of truth—of Nature, as it were—is at work mysteriously behind his consciousness, guiding his pen, without caring in the least whether the happy artist himself wanted to do the right thing or not."[8]

Still, Schenker found his Masters. In his discussion of the "scale-step" and "voice-leading," crucial in his analysis of tonal composition, Schenker noted: "The paragon of composition founded magnanimously and securely on the scale-steps (even in the fugues), whatever the audacity in voice-leading—the paragon of such composition, it seems to me, is still the work of Johann Sebastian Bach. What planning, what perspicuity, and what endurance!"[9]

The common picture of the Master or of the genius has two primary features. The genius is one who masters all rules or general principles of production quickly. In twentieth-century caricature, he is pictured at age five—somehow dressed in a Fauntleroy suit—being told by his Master Teacher, pointing to some door, "Go, I have nothing more to teach you!" But looking at the quality of his product, it is the second feature of the genius that appears to be the more important and that places the concept of genius squarely within Romantic philosophy. The rules or the principles of production do not provide for or secure the quality of the product of genius. The quality must be a result of transcending or the outright breaking of rules. Again, in twentieth-century caricature, the genius is pictured as one who violates even social rules of deportment; he is the proverbial Impossible Person who gets along with no one; in the Hollywood version, the genius throws things, generally made of porcelain, that smash dramatically on walls. Both of these traits of "genius" are easily traced to Western European German philosophers—to Kant, Hegel, Schopenhauer, and Nietzsche, who located meritorious artistic production in "freedom" from rule. In Kant's dictum, "genius gives the rule to art," even though he acknowledged that "in all free arts something of a compulsory character is still required. . . ."[10] The obvious question in this stress on artistic freedom is how, from such mode of production the work of genius is intelligible to others. Kant posited a solution in a theory of the relation between the imagination and understanding. Within his distinction between the "master" and "slave" moralities, on the other hand, Nietzsche denied general intelligibility. Products of genius were of the masters, for the masters.[11] Yet for Hegel, "the more exalted the rank of an artist, the more profoundly ought he to portray depths of soul and mind," which are "open to the channels of a universal experience."[12]

Perhaps greater detailing of psychological traits of genius will explain better how claims to universal understanding of the product of genius have been made. For Hegel, musical genius may be lacking in "intellectual conception" or "positive thought." Nietzsche's interpretation requires that the genius have "lived" and have "suffered." With this interpretation the product of genius is then looked at as an expression of personal suffering. This spelled Nietzsche's extension of Hegel's theory of the necessity of opposing forces of "life, experience" to "discipline" the "mind and heart" of the genius. Stated most extremely in his early work, *The Birth of Tragedy From the Spirit of Music,* Nietzsche later criticized his work as "smell[ing] offensively Hegelian."[14] But his stress at that point in his philosophical development upon the necessity of suffering, the identification of the primary genius as the musician, and the concept of genius as operating free from rule are all marks of Romantic philosophy that extended well into the twentieth century. J. W. N. Sullivan selected Beethoven as the top musical genius, and attempted in his book, *Beethoven: His Spiritual Development,* to correlate the deepening of "spiritual contexts" in Beethoven's compositions (culminating in the last quartets), with Beethoven's increased personal suffering. This necessitated an interpretation of Beethoven's compositions as *expressions* understandable universally. Thus: "The greater importance the world has always attributed to the third, fifth, seventh and ninth symphonies compared with the fourth, sixth and eighth, is not because of any purely musical superiority they possess, but because everyone is more or less clearly aware that greater issues are involved, that something more important for mankind is being expressed."[15]

Within this philosophical framework, it is interesting to note that Sullivan's descriptions of the consummate in Beethoven's compositions retains, albeit in a flamboyant Romantic manner, the same recognition of repetition of form, observed by Ingarden as an "essential agent" in Western European music. In describing the *Hammerklavier* sonata, Sullivan wrote: From the *Hammerclavier* sonata itself nothing more could come. Its spiritual content is at the end of a process, an end that contains within itself no new beginning. The completely naked Beethoven, relying upon nothing whatever but his inner resources, has said the last word in the *Hammerclavier* sonata. Without some new life added to him, without some new organization of his experience, the undying energy of the *Hammerclavier* fugue can be used only to say over again what it has already said."[16]

Of eighteenth- and nineteenth-century authors, probably Schopenhauer came the closest in his understanding of genius to what we shall here suggest. In *The World as Will and Idea*, Schopenhauer drew an unusual relation between genius and madness. Interestingly, he did not identify madness as irrationality, nor as not knowing the difference between what is true and what is not true. He found in madness a failure of memory. Thus, in people who are mad, "particular scenes of the past are known correctly, just like the particular present; but there are gaps in their recollection which they fill up with fictions. . . . If madness reaches a high degree, there is complete absence of memory, so that the madman is quite incapable of any reference to what is absent or past. . . . The knowledge of the madman has this in common with that of the brute, both are confined to the present."[17]

Theories of genius have not generally trafficked with memory. They have more consistently been related to "creativeness," "imagination," or other states of mind that are *active* agents of production. Kant described a state of mind that is "set in swing."[18] It is assumed, after all, to be the genius who "does it." Were it not for his mental-spiritual activity, we would have no remarkable products. Surely this is the reasonable conclusion in the space-time world as we know it. When musical or other artistic works are viewed as intentional objects, then the "choice and control of individuals," as Gurney put it, must be the primary determining factors to look at in explaining what is "marvellous" in art. We can, for the moment, bypass the question of why Schopenhauer spoke of memory as he did and also set music aside as *the* primary art. At least we can bypass the reasons he himself would have given. But we can begin a different locus of explanation by recalling Proust's observations about a madeleine dipped in tea and the looks of Combray.

Let us suppose that Proust's memory had not returned. Let us suppose that he experienced the "shudder" through his whole body and an "all-powerful joy" upon the moment "when the crumbs touched" his palate. In this situation, he would have been in great need of an explanation of what he experienced. Lacking the recall that he so graphically detailed, we can then posit that the remainder of the quotation in chapter one might read thus:

> Whence could it have come to me, this all-powerful joy? *Mon Dieu,* I exclaimed. Of course! It is this cake! This madeleine is truely *magnifique!* I must find the chef and get his recipe. But on the morrow, the chef shrugged his shoulders and informed me that he *had* no recipe. "I don't know *how* I do it," he said. "An egg here, a pinch of salt there. . . ." But you are a genius, I said. Don't you know that when I dip your cake into my tea, a shudder runs through my whole body, and I experience an all-powerful joy? Forthwith, I bought from him an entire case of his cake, and hurried home to taste it again in some freshly brewed tea. But, strangely, this time no shudder ran through my body and I experienced no joy. Was this chef an *imposteur?* Or perhaps he had baked these new crumbs on one of his off-days. Every genius has his off-days. No, Marcel, I concluded. It is the fault of your own taste buds. They are sated.

If, as was the case, Proust's memory *had* returned, then none of the above speculations would have been necessary, perhaps even thought of. But it would mean that the shudder and all-powerful joy were not results of anyone else's mental-spiritual activity. It would have been, in this case, the product of a happy accident in which no active human mind had a significant part. Lacking such a connection, we could explain Proust's joy in his recalled past without any recourse to a theory of expression, whether the expression be of a genius or of a mere baker of cake.

Let us extend this line of thinking, then, to a composer called by Hanslick "the greatest musical genius the world has ever seen."[19] What could Mozart have done in composing music that might trigger recall of something forgotten, yet something universally understood by all human beings and charged with emotion? Rather than thinking of Mozart as having a special capacity— musical genius—that most of us mere mortals do not have at all, might it be possible, following Schopenhauer's observations about memory, to think of Mozart as having an especially acute auditory memory that all of us share in some degree? Might it in this way be possible to trace claims to "universality" in music and to view Mozart not as a genius who, through some mysterious power, brought into being things that had not existed before, but as one adept at clearing away obstructions to anyone's auditory recall? Might it be possible in this way to point to products of "genius" that indeed break at least some culturally contingent rules of production, but that are still intelligible to others? Within this framework, Mozart would not be thought of as having *expressed* anything. He would have been doing something else. Carrying this to the above descriptions of Beethoven's music, J. W. N. Sullivan (similarly to Susanne Langer) made an observation of something that in fact happens, but mistakenly identified it as an expression.

This suggestion of replacing the concept of musical genius with that of another psychological activity is surely not intended as a complete replacement. Explication of the quality of depth via auditory recall does not account for the quality of "greatness"—a quality as often noted as the mark of musical genius, as is depth. Schenker's references to the "planning, perspicuity and endurance" of Bach more clearly link Bach's music to greatness than they do to depth. For Schenker, musical genius appears to have been identified primarily through structural, formal mastery, through what Hanslick called in general terms the "intellectual principle." This is quite different from Hegel's note that musical genius often operates prior to mental or intellectual development. On the other hand, the more greatness is stressed as the primary product of genius, the less likely it is that the genius will also be thought of primarily as one who breaks or transcends rules of composition.

When composers' works are monumental—both great and deep—the question of origin looms large; the location of the origin psychologically in something the composer was doing, thinking, or feeling seems most clearly justified. In an art that indisputably involves auditory memory, there has yet been an inability to point to anything outside the memory of the individual composer, to any common fund of human auditory experience that the composer, through his happy choices, might guide us to remember. In this regard, composition of spectacular musical works has probably been the most mysterious of all artistic production, and therefore the most in need of just such a concept as that of *genius* for its explanation. It also appears to be no accident that the two philosophers—both German—Schopenhauer and Nietzsche, whose understanding of genius also placed the musician as its best exemplar, did not detail the genius as the intellectual master of structural principles, but rather as the sufferer, the breaker of rules, the quasi-madman. Their interpretation appears to have stressed the quality of depth, as does also George Marek's observation about Beethoven, the genius, at the beginning of this chapter: The "spell" of Beethoven is compounded of our feeling that we will never understand his music to the full, will never plumb its depths, and yet that we do understand it very well. Our explication of depth metaphor in music criticism through a theory of partial recall in chapter one can, through such interpretations, thus connect with the concept of musical genius, without requiring a claim that the "genius" composer of "deep" music is *expressing* anything at all.

NOTES

1. "Some Remarks on Ingardenian Theory of a Musical Work," translated by Ursala Niklas, in *Roman Ingarden and Contemporary Polish Aesthetics*, edited by Piotr Graff and Slaw Krzemień-Ojak (Warsaw: Polish Academy of Sciences, Institute of Philosophy and Sociology, PWN, Polish Scientific Publishers, 1975), 129.

2. *"Uwagi do uwag Zofii Lissy,"* ["Some Remarks on Remarks of Zofia Lissa"], *Studia Estetyczne* 3 (1966):115-128.

3. Mark Brunswick, "Tonality and Perspective," *Musical Quarterly* 39 (1943):435.

4. *The Cognition of the Literary Work of Art,* translated by Ruth Ann Crowley and Kenneth R. Olson (Evanston, Ill.: Northwestern University Press, 1973), 206n.

5. *Harmony,* translated by Elisabeth Mann Borgese (Chicago: University of Chicago Press, 1954), 159, 235, 244, 245, 250, 254n, 273, 174.

6. Ibid., 250.

7. Ibid., 173.

8. Ibid., 60.

9. Ibid., 174.

10. *Critique of Judgment,¶* 43, translated by J. C. Meredith.

11. F. W. Nietzsche, *Genealogy of Morals,* translated by Walter Kaufmann and R. J. Hollingdale, (New York: Vintage Books, 1967).

12. G. W. F. Hegel, *The Philosophy of Fine Art,* translated by F. P. B. Osmaston, (New York: Hacker Art Books. 1975), I, 37, 64.

13. Ibid., 37.

14. F. W. Nietzsche, *Ecco Homo,* translated by Walter Kaufmann, (New York: Vintage Books, 1967).

15. J. W. N. Sullivan, *Beethoven: His Spiritual Development* (New York: Vintage Books, Random House, 1927), 103-104.

16. Ibid., 138.

17. Arthur Schopenhauer, *The World as Will and Idea,* translated by R. B. Haldane and J. B. Kemp, (London: Routledge & Kegan Paul; New York: Charles Scribner's Sons, 1950), I, 249.

18. *Critique of Judgment,* Book II, ¶ 49, 2nd paragraph: ". . . was die Gemütskräfte zweckmässig in Schwung versetzt . . ."

19. *The Beautiful in Music,* op. cit., 58.

Conclusion

In its empirical references, Western epistemology has not tradition-
ally differentiated between "sense perceptions" coming through
different sense media, although it now appears that empiricists
have really been talking almost exclusively about visual perceptions. Hence, the musical work that is known by audition has
been indiscriminately included in the world described by empiricists and not set aside as "not a real object" in accord with
Ingarden's conclusion. Similarly, in a general theory of value,
aesthetic theory, and philosophy of art, we typically find indis-
criminate references to any sense medium or to any art. It should
now be recognized that, in a serious way, this blanket treatment
of sense media has been a mistake. This is not to imply that
epistemology would have been better off to give special credence
to auditory perception, which might have led to a defense of
solipsism, or to a general denial of the subject-object, public-
private, or universal-particular dichotomies. But it is to suggest
that divisions between knowing and valuing might not have been
so strict and attempts to move from descriptions of the empirical
facts to their positive or negative evaluation would not have been
nearly so difficult. Thus, scientific theories might have had much
easier access to understanding an empirical world of delight, and
an easier time relating to religions where solipsism may not be
such a bad thing after all.

Visual perceptions are stable in a way that auditory perceptions are not. They can be made to stand still, can even be tied
together into another perception, i.e., of a sack, labeled "Class of
All Possible Perspectives." On the other hand, no sooner are
auditory perceptions heard than they vanish and their exact
recapture is immediately dependent upon memory. Had this

essential difference been in mind, epistemologists' neglect of memory might not have been nearly the scandal that C. I. Lewis found it to be. Aestheticians' inquiries into ontology of artworks might have avoided apparent reduction of all evaluations to descriptions. The clear suggestion from our inquiries is that the key to finding and explaining judgments of intrinsic value lies in separate study of auditory perception; that exclusive, or almost exclusive, concentration upon visual perception in a present-future orientation will likely lead only to where it already has led—to identification and explanation of what has been termed by Dewey, Beardsley, and others "instrumental," and by C. I. Lewis "extrinsic" value. And, as Stace clearly indicated, it is in identification of intrinsic value in something common to all humans that we find surest footing against relativism of value judgment in *empirical* matters.

Our study of auditory perception separately from visual/ tactual perception has led to refinement of reference of the particular valuational terms *depth* and *genius*. It now appears that depth-references in music criticism differ in a primary way from depth-references to visual or literary arts or to philosophy itself: They do not connote connection with wisdom such as would be acquired, as Arnheim put it, "through the ages," in experience of the space-time world that is primarily visual/tactual. Depth judgments of music appear in children very early, and no child is wise. As for the concept of genius, at least a partially different understanding is called for when genius is regarded as a capacity to produce "deep music." Where genius is linked to creativity, as Hofstadter indicated, depth is not created by an artist, but rather is *found* by "going backward." Thus, the Romantic interpretation of the artist as a "creator," who by a mysterious power "makes" whatever in his work is of aesthetic value, appears (in part at least) to be misguided. What we have taken to be a primary value of auditory art—the quality of depth—has been understood in such a way as to view the composer as a leader in auditory recognition and recall for everyone. To the extent that what is recalled is characteristic of all of human auditory experience, Romantic claims to universality of understanding through music still appear to be justified. And although our interpretation does not view the composer as achieving freedom through breaking rules of production, he still may be viewed as producing something that allows human beings a return to freedom in a much broader sense—freedom from the conflicts, the upsets, the threats of the spatial world.

From the point of view of empirical philosophy or of science, our explication of depth metaphor in music criticism may appear unsatisfactory on more than one count. There may be an expectation that the term "depth" be further clarified, further "unpacked." Yet there is a recalcitrance in this particular term toward this, reflected in the observation that depth is "something that I can't put my finger on." If we grasp this metaphor as accurate or revealing about the quality of depth, then further clarification of the term seems to be fairly precluded. Also, "clarification" generally proceeds within a physicalistic scheme such that we are expected to make it "clear" whether a term refers to a property of an object or to the feeling of a judge, in a context of an exclusive disjunction. Such an expectation precludes a possibility of clarifying the linguistic function of "deep" phenomenalistically.

Still more important, it may be expected that our so-called theory of partial recall be verifiable. From the empirical point of view how do we assess such a theory or tell whether, indeed, something like what we have argued is really going on when judgments of depth are made? This is not just a matter of not being able to refute a theory based on the idea of unconscious memory, but of not being able clearly to identify a confirmation. If the statement "All men are mortal" is not refutable either, it is at least easy to find confirmation of the statement as, one by one, we watch men die. A suggestion, however, that the Rastafarian in listening to reggae is retreating to a prenatal solipsistic state, through which he realizes that all men are brothers and are somehow at one with God, is lacking in the kind of immediate empirical evidence such as we have when we watch men die.

These problems must be acknowledged. The primary aim of our inquiry, however, has not been to convince the reader of the truth of a theory of partial recall of prenatal auditory existence. We have taken the *explanatory* power of the thesis to make it worth pursuing and taking seriously. Not only does it suggest answers to the questions listed at the end of chapter one, it suggests a reason why film music is consistently judged to be lacking in depth. It suggests an answer to a primary question arising from Ingarden's observations: How does it happen that a repetitious

structure that is foreign to literature and typically produces boredom quickly in visual arts is the very structure characterizing an
art whose immediate affective appeal seems to be strongest of
all? It suggests a reason why music is consistently praised as a
"universal language." Probably most important to philosophical
aestheticians, it suggests an explanation of why the primary critical
spatial metaphor of "depth" always functions in a valuational and
maximally positive way, and why its use always seems to have a
double reference, i.e., both to a property of an object judged and
to feelings of the judge. It does not appear that a physicalistic
philosophical scheme can explain the latter linguistic double function, and it does not appear that pragmatic inquiries into valuation, such as that of C. I. Lewis, promise from their present-future
orientation to answer the former question. The constant positive
valuational function of "deep" reduces at best only to a highly
probable prediction. Yet within our explanatory scheme we have
not had to go the route of the Platonist or of the mystic and say
that aesthetic value that humans find is independent of *all* sense
perception. We only have to say that some such value is independent of that *visual* perception that has dominated and simultaneously limited philosophers' inquiries in matters epistemological,
metaphysical, valuational, and/or psychological.

Especially through the influence of Wittgenstein, another
objection to our polemic may be raised. Our initial inquiry has
been based upon what may be regarded as a rather limited form
of language analysis in which we took the critical criterion of
"depth" to be a spatial metaphor and to function in a consistently
valuational and maximally positive way. But, it may be said, it is
naive to look for an explanation of this use. It is one thing to point
out or to analyze a particular use, and quite another to explain it.
If we know how to play a "language game," this is not to say that
the philosophical analyst has access to conditions of what is
recognized as a highly complex and socially dependent phenomenon. Such a view of language analysis, however, no more provides an account of the constant positive valuational use and
double function of the particular word "deep" in art criticism than
do physicalistic or pragmatic schemes. We should think, under a
condition of social contingency, that this word, as other valuational words, would sometimes function in contexts that are valuationally neutral or even negative. The word "unity" often is used in

a valuationally positive way, yet there are many instances in which pointing out "unity" is valuationally neutral or even sometimes negative, as when we complain that an art work is "too unified" and needs "variety." Thus, if "deep" (as a metaphor) has this peculiar consistent valuational and positive critical function, usual interpretations of language analysis leave us only puzzled. In this particular case, to resolve such puzzle or to account for the unusual behavior of this particular word, we have been forced into making *some kind of metaphysical and epistemological assumptions.* But perhaps most disturbing about hoped-for constructive progress in "aesthetic" matters via language analysis is that past inquiries into particular vocabulary—for example, into "unity," "structure," "expression" or "style"—have not left us any more enlightened about their valuational functions than they have about their nonvaluational ones. Perhaps the "enlightenment" we are presumed to have gained in carrying a Wittgensteinian torch has not moved beyond the early logical positivistists' conviction that valuational vocabulary belongs in the bin of "emotive language" and beyond the purview of analysis.

Well, then, perhaps we should abandon all attempts at analysis of valuation. Certainly, within boundaries of science we are tempted to move away from value judgments altogether in search of what is true and what is false about artistic production. Let the scientifically irresponsible wax enthusiastic about the remarkable, the great, the deep, or about "all the things that make life worth while." When Susanne Langer declared with conviction that in Western Europe "music has reached its highest development,"[1] we may then find her conviction gratuitous. When one inquires into different cultures as an anthropologist, one wants to give due credit to the particular value criteria of the particular culture. When one studies a particular art from an historical perspective of musicology, one looks for "authenticity" rather than for judgmental pedestals. Relativism from perspectives of anthropology or history is not only easy to come by, it also appears almost built into the method of a scholar who regards himself as a scientist. Our grounds against relativism of judgment in auditory art at least provide a basis, however, for sorting out what of Romantic philosophy may still be justified, what in the naturalism of John Dewey may be clearly wrong, and what in recent trends in language analysis is off a productive track.

Hegel drew a close relation between art, philosophy, and religion. As Morton White indicates, Dewey's stress on antidualism was clearly influenced by Hegel's metaphysical idealism in which the subject-object distinction is lost. Darwin also was useful for Dewey. Darwin "was instrumental in showing that there was something in common between the behavior and the development of human beings and nonhuman beings. This reinforced the metaphysical unity between humans and objects that Dewey took over from Hegel. Together, both oppositions to dualism lead to the belief in what Dewey later called 'the biological matrix' of all human behavior."[2] Had Dewey drawn significant differences between sensory media of the biological organism as did Gurney, he might have been able to bear out his antidualism within a biological matrix of immediate awareness. As it was, Dewey insisted that aesthetic values can only result from the challenges of "everyday experience," so that however "immediate" the "aesthetic" in experience resolving these challenges might be, however "fused" contributing biological-psychological functions in this experience might be, we do not have in Dewey's understanding an explanation of the quality of depth in auditory art nor an explanation of universality in any art in the literal sense in which we have taken it. Stace's criticism of Lewis should apply here to Dewey and other pragmatists as well. Perhaps most important, however, if our tracing of primary aesthetic value in auditory art is correct, then Dewey's essential thesis is simply false.

Throughout our excursions lies a demonstration of a need to separate auditory perception for study in a new way, independently of visual/tactual perception. Contrary to studies in search of principles relating to all "arts," to *any* "aesthetic" judgment or *any* sense medium, such study should demonstrate that all we really need is an understanding of one criterion related to one art and one sense medium, in order to break through the barrier to finding a long-sought universal grounding of valuation. In detail, such study should free a primary valuational criterion from confusion with the concept of "expression." It should give credence to passive as well as active functions of mind as significant contributors to aesthetic value in auditory art. It should free claims to universal understanding through music from counterclaims to contingent understanding in the space-time world. And it should enable us to argue against relativism of judgment in auditory art without abandoning a scientific stance. Clearly our inquiries extend in a number of directions: to epistemology, value theory, philosophy of mind (especially in concerns with memory and forgetting), social philosophy, and philosophy of religion. Further extensions, however, remain for other scholars to make.

NOTES

1. Susanne K. Langer, *Feeling and Form* (New York: Charles Scribner's Sons, 1953), 143.
2. Morton White, *The Origin of Dewey's Instrumentalism* (New York: Columbia University Press, 1943), 150-151.